REFRESHING PUNCH

Enjoy With Amazing Punch Recipes

Steve Potter

© **Copyright 2021**

The content contained within this book may not be reproduced, duplicated or transmitted without direct written permission from the author or the publisher.

Under no circumstances will any blame or legal responsibility be held against the publisher, or author, for any damages, reparation, or monetary loss due to the information contained within this book. Either directly or indirectly.

Legal Notice:

This book is copyright protected. This book is only for personal use. You cannot amend, distribute, sell, use, quote or paraphrase any part, or the content within this book, without the consent of the author or publisher.

Disclaimer Notice:

Please note the information contained within this document is for educational and entertainment purposes only. All effort has been executed to present accurate, up to date, and reliable, complete information. No warranties of any kind are declared or implied. Readers acknowledge that the author is not engaging in the rendering of legal, financial, medical or professional advice. The content within this book has been derived from various sources. Please consult a licensed professional before attempting any techniques outlined in this book.

By reading this document, the reader agrees that under no circumstances is the author responsible for any losses, direct or indirect, which are incurred as a result of the use of information contained within this document, including, but not limited to, — errors, omissions, or inaccuracies.

CONTENTS

- WATERMELON PUNCH 1
- WHAT HIT ME PUNCH 2
- WHISKY PUNCH 3
- WHITE GRAPE~ TANGERINE~ & ASTI-SPUMANTE PUNCH 4
- WHITE HOUSE PINK FRUIT PUNCH 5
- WHITE SANGRIA PUNCH (NONALCHOLIC) 6
- WHITE WINE PUNCH 7
- YELLOW FRUIT PUNCH 8
- "NO PUNCH" CHAMPAGNE 9
- "STING-LIKE-A-BEE" PUNCH 10
- 1, 2, 3, PUNCH 11
- 4-FRUIT WEDDING PUNCH 12
- 7-UP PUNCH YIELD 14
- ALKOHOLFREIER PLANTER'S PUNCH 15
- ALOHA FRUIT PUNCH 16
- BRANDY MILK PUNCH 17
- BRIDAL FRUIT PUNCH (NON-ALCOHOLIC) 18
- BRIDAL SWEET PUNCH 19
- BRIDES LUNCH PUNCH 20
- BROWN COW PUNCH 21
- BUBBLING JADE PUNCH 22
- CANADIAN PUNCH 23

- CARIBBEAN GUAVA PUNCH 24
- CHAMPAGNE FRUIT PUNCH 25
- CHAMPAGNE PUNCH 26
- CHATHAM ARTILLERY PUNCH 28
- CHEERY CHERRY PUNCH 29
- CHERRY TEA PUNCH 30
- CHOCOLATE PUNCH 31
- CHRISTMAS CHERRY BERRY PUNCH 32
- CHRISTMAS CRANBERRY PUNCH 34
- CHRISTMAS PARTY PUNCH 35
- CHRISTMAS RUM PUNCH 36
- CHRISTMAS SNOW PUNCH 37
- CIDER AND BRANDY PUNCH 38
- CIDER FRUIT PUNCH A LA NORMANDE 39
- CIDER PUNCH YIELD 41
- CINNAMON CANDY PUNCH 42
- CINNAMON TEA PUNCH 43
- CITRUS CHAMPAGNE PUNCH 44
- CITRUS FRUIT PUNCH 45
- CITRUS MINT PUNCH 46
- CITRUS PUNCH YIELD 47
- CITRUS SPARKLER PUNCH 48
- CITRUS TEA PUNCH WITH FRESH MINT 49
- CLARENCE MOODY'S HOLIDAY PUNCH 51
- CLARET PUNCH 52
- COCA-COLA PUNCH 53
- COCONUT RUM PUNCH 54
- COFFEE CHOCOLATE PUNCH 55

- COFFEE EGGNOG PUNCH 56
- COFFEE MOCHA PUNCH 57
- COFFEE POT PUNCH 59
- COFFEE PUNCH 60
- COFFEE VANILLA PUNCH 61
- COFFEE-KAHLUA PUNCH 62
- COLD KAHLUA COFFEE PUNCH 63
- COLLEGE PUNCH YIELD 64
- CORAL PUNCH 65
- COWBOY PUNCH YIELD 66
- CRAN-ORANGE PUNCH 67
- CRANBERRY HOLIDAY PUNCH 68
- CRANBERRY LEMON PUNCH 69
- CRANBERRY LIME NONALCOHOLIC PUNCH 70
- CRANBERRY ORANGE PUNCH 71
- CRANBERRY ORANGE TEA PUNCH 72
- CRANBERRY PARTY PUNCH 74
- CRANBERRY VODKA PUNCH 75
- CRANBERRY ZINFANDEL PUNCH 76
- CRANBERRY-CIDER PUNCH 77
- CRANBERRY-LEMON PUNCH 78
- CRANBERRY-PEACH PUNCH 79
- CRANBERRY-WINE PUNCH 80
- CRANBERRY/RASPBERRY PUNCH 81
- CREAMY PINEAPPLE PUNCH 82
- CREAMY PUNCH YIELD 83
- CREOLE COFFEE ICE CREAM PUNCH 84
- CROCKED PUNCH 85

- DAIQUIRI PUNCH YIELD 86
- DEES' VODKA PUNCH 87
- DELICIOUS COFFEE PUNCH 88
- DELICIOUS PARTY PUNCH 89
- DELICIOUS SUMMER PUNCH 90
- DELORES'S PUNCH 91
- DESMOND'S RUM PUNCH 92
- DISHWATER PUNCH 93
- DOTS PUNCH YIELD 94
- DOUBLE SHERBET PUNCH 95
- DREAMSICLE PUNCH 96
- DUDLEY EPPEL'S HOT CIDER-CRANBERRY PUNCH 97
- EASY PARTY PUNCH 98
- EASY PUNCH YIELD 99
- ELLY MAY'S WEDDING PUNCH 100
- EMERIL'S FROZEN MILK PUNCH 1 101
- ERDBEER BOWLE (STRAWBERRY WINE PUNCH) 102
- EVERGREEN MINT PUNCH 104
- EYE OPENERS - MILK PUNCH 105
- FABULOUS FRUIT PUNCH 106
- FABULOUS PUNCH (NO SUGAR) 107
- FALL PUNCH YIELD 108
- PUNCH 110
- FELINE PUNCH 111
- FESTIVE PUNCH YIELD 112
- FIRECRACKER PUNCH 113
- FIRESIDE PUNCH YIELD 114
- FISH HOUSE PUNCH 115

- FIVE FRUIT PUNCH 116
- FLAVOR-PACKED FRUIT PUNCH 118
- FRESH FRUIT PUNCH 119
- FROSTED FRUIT PUNCH 120
- FROSTY PINK PUNCH 121
- FROZEN PUNCH 122
- FROZEN RUM PUNCH 123
- FRUIT JUICE PUNCH 124
- FRUIT MEDLEY PUNCH 125
- FRUIT MEDLEY PUNCH WITH DELLA ROBBIA ICE RING 126
- FRUIT PUNCH YIELD 128
- FRUIT TEA PUNCH 129
- FRUITY ISLAND PUNCH 130
- FRUITY SHERBET PUNCH 131
- GALA FRUIT PUNCH 132
- GARDEN PUNCH 133
- GARDEN TEA PUNCH 134
- GENEVA'S PARTY PUNCH 137
- GIBBSVILLE'S PUNCH 138
- GINGER ALE PUNCH 139
- GINGER ALE-SHERBET PUNCH 140
- GINGER AND BLOOD ORANGE PUNCH 141
- GINGER APPLE FRUIT PUNCH 143
- GINGER TROPICAL PUNCH 145
- GLORIA'S PUNCH 147
- GLORIOUS CHRISTMAS PUNCH 148
- GLUGG "HOLIDAY" PUNCH 149
- GOLDEN AZTEC PUNCH 151

- GOLDEN GATE PUNCH 152
- GOLDEN GLOW PUNCH 153
- GOLDEN PUNCH 154
- GOLDEN SUMMER FRUIT PUNCH 155
- GOLDEN SUMMER PUNCH 156
- GOLLEEE GELATIN PUNCH 157
- GRADUATION PUNCH 158
- GRANNY'S HONEY PARTY PUNCH 159
- GRANNY'S PUNCH 160
- GRAPEFRUIT-STRAWBERRY PUNCH 161
- GREEN PUNCH 162
- GUAVA PUNCH 163
- HALLOWEEN PUNCH 164
- HARBOUR ISLAND RUM PUNCH 165
- HARVEST PUNCH 166
- HAWAIIAN LUAU PUNCH 167
- HAWAIIAN PUNCH 168
- HEALTH-KICK PUNCH 169
- HIBISCUS TEA PUNCH 170
- HILTON PUNCH 171
- HOLIDAY DELIGHT PUNCH 172
- HOLIDAY DRINKS - BRANDY MILK PUNCH 173
- HOLIDAY FRUIT PUNCH 174
- HOLIDAY PUNCH 176
- HOMECOMING PARTY PUNCH (SERVES 100) 177
- HOT "TAILGATE" PUNCH 178
- HOT BUTTERED PUNCH 179
- HOT CHRISTMAS PUNCH 180

- OT CIDER PUNCH 181
- HOT CRANBERRY PUNCH 182
- HOT FRUIT PUNCH 183
- HOT HOLIDAY PUNCH 184
- HOT MILK PUNCH 185
- HOT MULLED FRUIT PUNCH 186
- HOT OR COLD PERKY PUNCH 187
- HOT PINEAPPLE PUNCH 188
- HOT PUNCH 189
- HOT SCARLET WINE PUNCH 190
- HOT SPICED CRANBERRY PUNCH 191
- HOT SPICED FRUIT PUNCH 193
- HOT SPICED PERCOLATOR PUNCH 194
- HOT SPICED PUNCH 195
- HOT SPICY LEMONADE PUNCH 196
- HOT WEATHER PUNCH 197
- HOT WHISKEY PUNCH 198
- HOT WINE CRANBERRY PUNCH 199
- ORANGE-PEACH PARTY PUNCH 200
- IRISH COFFEE-EGGNOG PUNCH 202
- ISLAND FRUIT PUNCH 204
- ISLAND RUM PUNCH 205
- JACK CONNOR'S ARTILLERY PUNCH 206
- JAMAICAN RUM PUNCH 207
- JANE GLASS' PUNCH 208
- JELLO PUNCH 209
- JUBILEE PUNCH YIELD 12 210

REFRESHING PUNCH

➤ WATERMELON PUNCH

Yield 1 Servings

- 1 c sugar
- 1 c water
- 1/2 sm evenly-shaped watermelon
- 1/4 c brandy
- 1 cn (12 oz) lemon-lime soda
- 1 ice cubes
- 1 t pine nuts, Shelled

In a saucepan, bring sugar and water to a boil; cool. Scoop watermelon with a melon baller; discard seeds. Pour sugar syrup over watermelon balls. Scoop remaining watermelon; squeeze in a clean cloth to extract juice. Combine watermelon balls, watermelon juice, and brandy; chill. Cut the upper edge of the watermelon shell in a saw-tooth design and use as a punch bowl. Just before serving, add watermelon mixture, soda, and ice cubes to watermelon shell. Sprinkle with nuts. Makes 10 to 12 servings.

REFRESHING PUNCH

➤ WHAT HIT ME PUNCH

Yield 1 Servings

1. Put 1 12oz can each of orange juice, lemonade, pineapple juice w/ 16 oz can of limeade in large punch bowl.

Add 1 bottle of Everclear (or for those lightweights, vodka can be used).

3. Add enough ice to fill punchbowl, garnish with sliced oranges and mint leaves and serve.

REFRESHING PUNCH

➤ WHISKY PUNCH

Yield 1 Servings

- ❖ 3 lemons
- ❖ 1/2 lb sugar
- ❖ 2 pt water, Boiling
- ❖ 1 bottle scotch whisky

Peel the lemons finely and squeeze out the juice, then add peel and juice to the sugar in a large jug or bowl. Pour the boiling water over the lemons and sugar and leave until cold.

Strain into a large bowl and add the bottle of Scotch whisky, stirring well. Chill for at least an hour before serving.

REFRESHING
PUNCH

➤ WHITE GRAPE~ TANGERINE~ & ASTI-SPUMANTE PUNCH

Yield 12 Servings

- ❖ 48 oz white grape juice -unsweetened
- ❖ 6 oz tangerine juice concentrate
- ❖ 1 c club soda,chilled
- ❖ 1/4 c lemon juice
- ❖ 1/4 c brandy
- ❖ 1 champagne,domestic,chilled
- ❖ 1 orange slice,thin

In a punch bowl, whisk together the grape juice, tangerine concentrate, club soda, lemon juice, and brandy; cover and chill the mixture until cold. Add the champagne just before serving in punch glasses.

REFRESHING PUNCH

➤ WHITE HOUSE PINK FRUIT PUNCH

Yield 16 Servings

- ❖ 1 qt orange juice
- ❖ 2 c pineapple juice
- ❖ 1 1/2 qt cranberry juice
- ❖ 1 qt ginger ale
- ❖ 1 lock ice

In a large punch bowl, mix together fruit juices; chill. Just before serving, add ginger ale and stir.

Add ice. (Ice cubes make punch difficult to serve; use larger blocks of ice instead.) Ladle punch into pretty punch glasses, and garnish with orange slices, if desired.

Yield 12 to 16 servings

REFRESHING PUNCH

➤ WHITE SANGRIA PUNCH (NONALCHOLIC)

Yield 12 Servings

- ❖ 4 c white grape juice
- ❖ 1 c pink grapefruit juice
- ❖ 1 T lime juice
- ❖ 1 club soda,bottle, 750 ml -chilled
- ❖ 1 pink grapefruit,Slices

In large pitcher, combine grape, grapefruit and lime juices; refrigerate. Just before serving, add soda water and grapefruit slices.
MAKES 12 SERVINGS

REFRESHING
PUNCH

➤ WHITE WINE PUNCH

Yield 12 Servings

- ❖ 1 sm honeydew melon
- ❖ 1 lb watermelon
- ❖ 1 sm cantaloupe
- ❖ 20 oz dry white table wine
- ❖ 20 oz sweet Riesling wine
- ❖ 32 oz Moscato d'Asti wine
- ❖ 12 red grapes, sliced in half

Using 3 different sizes of melon ballers, measuring from 1/3- to 7/8-inch in diameter, scoop the melons into balls. Place the melon balls onto a baking pan, taking care to see that they don't touch one another.

Freeze until solid, 2 to 3 hours or overnight.

Mix the wines in a punch bowl. Add the grape halves and frozen melon balls, and serve.

This recipe yields 12 servings.

REFRESHING PUNCH

➤ YELLOW FRUIT PUNCH

Yield 96 Servings

- ❖ 1 cn (12-oz) orange juice,Frozen
- ❖ 1 cn (46-oz) orange-grapefruit -juice
- ❖ 1 cn (large) pineapple juice
- ❖ 1 maraschino cherries
- ❖ 1 pineaple,Crushed
- ❖ 3 qt ginger ale
- ❖ 1 bottle lemon juice
- ❖ 1 cn (46-oz) orange juice
- ❖ 1 lemon
- ❖ 1 orange
- ❖ 1 mint leaves

Mix juices and ginger ale together. Slice lemon and orange in slices and put the slices, cherries, crushed pineapple and mint leaves in. Makes 96 4-oz servings.

REFRESHING PUNCH

➤ "NO PUNCH" CHAMPAGNE

Yield 1 Servings

- ❖ 25 3/8 oz alcohol-free white wine -chilled
- ❖ 32 oz ginger ale,chilled
- ❖ 1 lemon,scored and thinly -- sliced,for garnish
- ❖ 1 lime,scored and thinly -- sliced,for garnish

Pour wine and ginger ale into 2-quart pitcher; mix well. Pour into glasses; garnish with fruit slices, if desired. Serve immediately. Yield seven (1-Cup) servings.

REFRESHING PUNCH

➤ "STING-LIKE-A-BEE" PUNCH

Yield 20 Servings

- ❖ 46 oz Apricot Nectar
- ❖ 46 oz Pineapple Juice
- ❖ 6 oz Concentrated Orange, Frozen -Juice
- ❖ 2 l Ginger Ale

Combine first three ingredients, then add ginger ale. Gently add as much chipped ice as container will allow.

REFRESHING PUNCH

➤ 1, 2, 3, PUNCH

Yield 1 Servings

- ❖ 26 z rye --
- ❖ 2 bottles sherry
- ❖ 3 bottles ginger ale
- ❖ 2 whole oranges --,Sliced

Pour 2 bottles of the ginger ale into a bundt pan and add some of the orange slices. Freeze and use as ice ring as it doesn't dilute the punch when it melts. Punch does become smoother as the ring melts. Put orange slices in the punch bowl and add other ingredients. (You may wish to have one more bottle of ginger ale to make the ice ring.)

REFRESHING PUNCH

➤ 4-FRUIT WEDDING PUNCH

Yield 1 Servings

- ❖ 2 parts orange juice
- ❖ 2parts lemonade
- ❖ 1part pineapple juice
- ❖ 1part grapefruit juice
- ❖ -(optional,but gives a nice
- ❖ ONE BATCH ACCORDING TO MOM ======
- ❖ 1 qt lemonade from a mix -prepared
- ❖ 1 cn (12-oz) orange juice,Frozen - reconstituted
- ❖ 1/2 tall can pineapple,Frozen -juice,reconstituted
- ❖ 1/2 tall can grapefruit juice -reconstituted (optional)

This recipe contains no carbonation and no ice cream. I have not tried it spiked, but you could probably add rum to it). This is our family's punch recipe--we serve it for all special occasions.

Prepare lemonade. Reconstitute orange juice, pineapple juice,and

REFRESHING
PUNCH

grapefruit juice, according to package directions, and in separate containers. Add lemonade to punch bowl. Add all of the orange juice, ½ (up to 3/4) of the pineapple juice, and 1/2 of the grapefruit juice.

Slice thin orange wheels and float on top for a festive look. Cherries would also look nice.

REFRESHING
PUNCH

➤ 7-UP PUNCH YIELD

1 Servings

- ❖ 1 cn 46-oz pineapple juice
- ❖ 1   juice of 2 lemons
- ❖ 2 c orange juice
- ❖ 1 mint leaves
- ❖ 6c water
- ❖ 4c sugar
- ❖ 4 bananas, mashed
- ❖ 1 7-up to stretch it
- ❖ 1 pk strawberries, Frozen

Mix sugar and water. Chill. Add fruit juices. Add bananas right away. (That is, don't let the mashed bananas sit.) Freeze. When ready to serve, break up the frozen base into pieces. Add strawberries and enough 7-Up to stretch.

REFRESHING
PUNCH

➤ ALKOHOLFREIER PLANTER'S PUNCH

- ❖ 1 2 cl grenadinesirup
- ❖ 12 cl zitronensaft
- ❖ 16 cl ananassaft ungesuesst
- ❖ 16 cl orangensaft
- ❖ 16 cl maracujanektar

Alle Zutaten mit Eis im Shaker schuetteln (oder in einem Glas gut verruehren) und auf Eis in ein grosses Glas giessen.

REFRESHING PUNCH

➤ALOHA FRUIT PUNCH

Yield 10 Servings

- ❖ 3/4 c water
- ❖ 1 t ginger root, chopped
- ❖ c guava juice
- ❖ 1 1/2 T lemon juice
- ❖ 1 1/2 c pineapple, finely chopped
- ❖ 1 c sugar

Add 1/4 cup water to ginger root. Boil 3 minutes. Strain. Add the liquid to the guava, lemon and pineapple juices. Make a syrup of sugar and remaining water. Cool. Combine with juices and pineapple. Chill t

REFRESHING PUNCH

➤ BRANDY MILK PUNCH

Yield 1 Servings

- 1 t sugar, confectioners
- 1 T creme de cacao, white
- 3/4 c whipping cream
- 1 1/2 oz brandy
- 1/2 c ice, crushed
- 1 ds nutmeg

Place sugar, creme de cocoa, cream and brandy in a cocktail shaker with crushed ice (regular cubes are fine, too). Shake briefly (longer if using cubes) and strain into an old fashioned glass. Garnish with nutmeg.

REFRESHING PUNCH

➤ BRIDAL FRUIT PUNCH (NON-ALCOHOLIC)

Yield 20 Servings

- ❖ 4 c tropical fruit juice (or -pink) - lemona,de
- ❖ 1cn strawberry juice,Frozen
- ❖ -concentrate, (280 ml)
- ❖ 3 c ginger ale
- ❖ 2 c soda water

In punch bowl, mix together fruit juice and juice concentrate. Pour ginger ale and soda water down side of bowl to avoid loss of carbonation. Serve over ice.

Makes about 10 cups or about 20 servings. Notes* Garnish the punch bowl with ice cubes and sprigs of fresh mint; for a fancier touch, use a ring mould to make a fruited ice ring.

REFRESHING PUNCH

➤ BRIDAL SWEET PUNCH

Yield 48 Servings

- ❖ 10 tea bags
- ❖ 3 c sugar
- ❖ 3 c orange juice
- ❖ 3 c pineapple juice, unsweetened
- ❖ 1 c lemon juice, fresh, strained
- ❖ 2 qt ginger ale
- ❖ GARNISH
- ❖ 1 mint leaves

This punch can be made in advance in large quantities.

Bring the water to a boil, add the tea bags and steep for 5 minutes. Remove the tea bags, add the sugar, mix and chill for at least 3 hours. Place the chilled tea in a punch bowl, add the juices, and stir. Just before serving, add the ginger ale and stir. Add some ice cubes and garnish with mint leaves.

REFRESHING PUNCH

➤ BRIDES LUNCH PUNCH

Yield 172 Servings

- ❖ 6 boxes lemon gelatin powder-3 oz. each
- ❖ 6 c hot water
- ❖ 12 qt water
- ❖ 24 qt pineapple juice
- ❖ 3 qt lemon juice
- ❖ 12 qt ginger ale
- ❖ 12 c sugar

Melt lemon jello in hot water.

Mix all ingredients except ginger ale and chill. Add ginger ale before serving

REFRESHING PUNCH

➤ BROWN COW PUNCH

Yield 1 Servings

- ❖ 2 qt chocolate milk
- ❖ 1/4 t almond extract
- ❖ 1/2 ga coffee ice cream

In a punch bowl, combine milk and extract. Add ice cream by scoopfuls and allow to float on top of punch. Or scoop ice cream into glasses; combine milk and extract, then pour over ice cream. Yield 3 quarts. Editor's note If coffee ice cream is unavailable, dissolve 2 teaspoons instant coffee granules in 2 teaspoons hot water and stir into vanilla ice cream.

REFRESHING PUNCH

➤ BUBBLING JADE PUNCH

Yield 1 Servings

- ❖ 2 pk Lime Gelatin,(3 oz. each)
- ❖ 2 c Water,Boiling
- ❖ 4 c Cold Water
- ❖ 12 oz Lemonade Concentrate,Frozen - and undiluted,Thawed
- ❖ 2 c Pineapple Juice
- ❖ 2 l Ginger Ale

Dissolve gelatin in boiling water; stir in cold water, lemonade concentrate, and pineapple juice; chill well. Don't chill too long or it solidifies!! Add ginger ale before serving.

REFRESHING PUNCH

➤ CANADIAN PUNCH

Yield 20 Servings

- ❖ 10 oz lemon juice
- ❖ 2 oz lime juice
- ❖ 21/2 oz grenadine
- ❖ 1 2   sugar
- ❖ 6oz welches grape juice, pink if - possible
- ❖ 1qt canadian whiskey
- ❖ 6 oz rum
- ❖ 2 qt sparkling water
- ❖ 1 qt cranberry juice

Combine all ingredients in a large punch bowl. Add ice and decorate withorange slices, cherries, etc. Serves 20. Perfect for holiday parties.

REFRESHING PUNCH

➤ CARIBBEAN GUAVA PUNCH

Yield 20 Servings

- ❖ 2 qt jamacian rum
- ❖ 1 1/2 c key lime juice
- ❖ 2 1/2 lb sugar (or less)
- ❖ 2 qt strong tea
- ❖ 1 qt sherry (sweet)
- ❖ 2 qt water
- ❖ 1 lb guava jelly
- ❖ 1/2 pt brandy
- ❖ 3 qt gingerale

Mix all ingredients in a very large punchbowl except the gingerale. Add gingerale just before serving time. Add ice cubes to suit.

Makes about 20 servings.

REFRESHING
PUNCH

➤ CHAMPAGNE FRUIT PUNCH

Yield 20 Servings

- 1   fifth sauterne, chilled
- 1   fifth champagne, chilled
-   2 c stemmed, washed
- 1 strawberries
- 2 qt grapefruit soda (wink or -squirt), chilled

Combine sauterne, champagne & soda in punch bowl. Drop in strawberries.

Makes 18-20 servings.

REFRESHING PUNCH

➤CHAMPAGNE PUNCH

Yield 20 Servings

- ❖ 1 cn (12-oz.) lemonade,Frozen -concentrat,e, undiluted
- ❖ 1cn (12-oz.) orange juice,Frozen - concen,trate, undiluted
- ❖ 2 c white grape juice
- ❖ 2 l white soda
- ❖ 2 bottles champagne
- ❖ -(recommend dry white vari
- ❖ 1 cn (large) pineapple juice
- ❖ -frozen into a mold
- ❖ 6 lemon slices,(optional)
- ❖ 6 orange slices,(optional)

Use a bundt cake pan to freeze your pineapple juice into the shape of a festive wreath to float in your punch bowl. Or, if you don't happen to have a bundt cake pan handy, you may want to add a half-cherry to each compartment of an ice cube tray to freeze your pineapple juice.

REFRESHING
PUNCH

Mix lemonade, orange juice, white grape juice, white soda, and champagne in punch bowl. Add frozen pineapple ring to chill 15 minutes prior to serving.

Garnish with lemon and orange slices, if desired.

REFRESHING PUNCH

➤ CHATHAM ARTILLERY PUNCH

Yield 1 Servings

- ❖ 1 1/2 ga catawba wine
- ❖ 1 1/2 qt rye whisky
- ❖ 1/2 ga st. croix rum 1/2 pt benedictine
- ❖ 1 qt brandy
- ❖ 1 1/2 ga strong tea
- ❖ 2 1/2 pk brown sugar
- ❖ 1 1/2   dozen oranges, juiced
- ❖ 1 1/2   dozen lemon, juiced

REFRESHING PUNCH

➤ CHEERY CHERRY PUNCH

Yield 60 Servings

- 3 pk cherry-flavored gelatin, 3oz - each
- 2 to 3 c sugar
- 6 c water, Boiling
- 46 oz can unsweetened pineapple -juice
- 12 oz can orange juice, Frozen -concentrate, thaw
- 12 oz lemonade concentrate, Frozen - thaw
- 1 ga cold water
- 2 bottles ginger ale, 2 liters - each

Dissolve gelatin and sugar in boiling water. Add pineapple juice, concentrates and cold water; mix well. Freeze, Just before serving, add ginger ale and mix well.

REFRESHING PUNCH

➤ CHERRY TEA PUNCH

Yield 10 Servings

- ❖ 1 c cherries
- ❖ 1/2 c sugar
- ❖ 2 c ,water
- ❖ 1c tea
- ❖ 1 c orange juice
- ❖ 1 c pineapple juice
- ❖ 1 qt ginger ale

Pit the cherries and place in a blender; pure and set aside. Combine the sugar and water; boil for five minutes, then cool. Add the pured cherries, tea, orange juice and pineapple juice; chill. Just before serving, pour into a punch bowl and add the ginger ale. Float a fruited ice ring on top.

Fruited Ice Ring Arrange whole cherries and orange slices in the bottom of a ring mold. Pour in just enough water to cover the fruit. Freeze until firm. Add cold water to fill the mold. Freeze again until firm.

REFRESHING PUNCH

➤ CHOCOLATE PUNCH

Yield 12 Servings

- ❖ 4 1-oz sq semisweet chocolate
- ❖ 1/2 c sugar
- ❖ 2 c hot water
- ❖ 2 qt milk
- ❖ 1 1/2 t vanilla extract
- ❖ 1 qt vanilla ice cream
- ❖ 1 qt club soda
- ❖ 1/2 pt heavy cream, whipped
- ❖ 1 cinnamon, Ground

Recipe by Spoonbread & Strawberry Wine - ISBN 0-385-47270-6 In a large saucepan combine the chocolate and sugar with the hot water. Bring to a boil, stirring for 2 mins. Add milk, and continue heating.

When hot, beat in vanilla with a rotary egg beater or whisk. Remove from heat. Chill, then pour into a punch bowl over ice cream. For sparkle, add club soda. Top with whipped cream and dust with cinnamon. Yield 12 servings.

REFRESHING
PUNCH

➤ CHRISTMAS CHERRY BERRY PUNCH

Yield 1 Servings

- ❖ 1 red maraschino cherries -well,Drained
- ❖ 1 green maraschino cherries -well,Drained
- ❖ 1 pk cherry gelatin,3 oz
- ❖ 1 c water,boiling
- ❖ 1 cn lemonade concentrate,Frozen - 6 oz
- ❖ 4 c cranberry juice cocktail
- ❖ 3 c water
- ❖ 1bottle ginger ale
- ❖ 1 liter -chilled

At least 1 day before serving, arrange red and green cherries in clusters in a ring mold that fits into your punch bowl.

Add water to just cover cherries. Freeze for about hours or till firm. Add more water to fill ring.

REFRESHING PUNCH

Freeze.

(If you don't have a punch bowl, freeze cherries in ice cube trays to float in a pitcher or individual glasses or cups.)

In a large heatproof pitcher or bowl, dissolve gelatin in boiling water. Add the lemonade concentrate, stirring to melt.

Add the cranberry juice and 3 cups water. Cover and chill.

Remove ice ring from mold by running warm water over it. Place in punch bowl, cherry side up.

Pour punch mixture over ice. Slowly pour in ginger ale.

Makes about 13 cups.

REFRESHING PUNCH

➤ CHRISTMAS CRANBERRY PUNCH

Yield 16 Servings

- ❖ 4 c cranberry juice cocktail
- ❖ 2 c orange juice
- ❖ 12 oz sugar-free lemon-lime pop
- ❖ 1 whole cranberries

Combine the cranberry and orange juices in a punch bowl. Pour the carbonated beverage down the sides of the bowl. Float whole cranberries on the top.

REFRESHING PUNCH

➤ CHRISTMAS PARTY PUNCH

Yield 50 Servings

- 1 cn (12-oz) orange juice,Frozen -concent,rate
- 1 cn (6-oz) lemonade,Frozen -concentrate
- 1 cn (18-oz) pineapple juice
- 6 c water
- 6 pt cranberry juice cocktail

Add water to frozen concentrates as directed on cans. Mix all ingredients well. Serve in punch bowl over ice. Yield 50 servings.

REFRESHING PUNCH

➤ CHRISTMAS RUM PUNCH

Yield 1 Servings

- 1 measure of fresh lime juice
- 2 measures of grenadine
- 3 measures of dark rum
- 4 measures of soda water
- 1 ds angostura bitters
- 1   nutmeg,Freshly Grated
- 1   ice

Fill the glass with ice and add a dash of the bitters.

Fill with the rest of the ingredients and then grate a little nutmeg on top.

REFRESHING PUNCH

➤ CHRISTMAS SNOW PUNCH

Yield 6-8 Servings

- ❖ 1 cn (46 ounces) hi-c hula punch - thorou,ghly chilled
- ❖ 2 pt vanilla ice cream,softened
- ❖ 2 c sprite,chilled

In punch bowl, combine Hi-C Hula Punch, Sprite and ice cream. Stir until well blended and chill. Makes 32 servings.

REFRESHING PUNCH

➤ CIDER AND BRANDY PUNCH

Yield 1 Servings

- 1 lemon and 1 orange, zest of
- 1 1/2 pt dry strong cider
- 1 oz soft brown sugar
- 2 cinnamon sticks
- 4 cloves
- 2 blades of mace, dried
- 1 1 inch slice root ginger -peeled
- 1 t nutmeg, Grated
- 3 T brandy
- 2 apples, cored and sliced

Put the lemon and orange zest, cider, sugar and spices into a deep-sided pan and warm through for about 10 minutes. Add the brandy and reheat gently. Serve with sliced fresh apples.

REFRESHING
PUNCH

➤ CIDER FRUIT PUNCH A LA NORMANDE

Yield 18 Servings

- ❖ 2 qt sparkling cider
- ❖ 1 pt carbonated water
- ❖ 1/2 c benedictine
- ❖ 1/2 c applejack
- ❖ 1 dozen thinly,Sliced
- ❖ 1 orange slices,halved
- ❖ 1 c hulled,washed fresh
- ❖ 1 small strawberries
- ❖ 1/3 c red maraschino,Chopped
- ❖ 1 cherries
- ❖ 1 lg chunk of ice

Have all the ingredients well chilled in advance. Combine cider and carbonated water in a large mixing bowl; add ice, and pour over ice

REFRESHING PUNCH

Benedictine and applejack. Whirl the ice chunk till mixture is well chilled; discard the ice and add orange slices, strawberries, and cherries. Serve in Chilled punch glasses.

REFRESHING PUNCH

➤ CIDER PUNCH YIELD

36 Servings

- 1 l cider
- 3 T brandy
- 200 ml lemonade 500 ml apple juice
- 4 cinnamon sticks
- 1 orange
- 10 cloves
- 2 T brown sugar
- 1 lemon, sliced
- 1 apple, cut into segments

In a large pan, slowly heat the liquids. Do not allow to boil. Add the cinnamon sticks. Pierce the orange with the cloves and cut the orange in half. Add the orange, sugar, lemon slices and apple to the punch.

Simmer for 40 minutes before serving.

REFRESHING PUNCH

➤ CINNAMON CANDY PUNCH

Yield 5 Servings

- 1 c water
- 1/2 c sugar
- 6 T cinnamon decorator candies
- 92 oz unsweetened pineapple juice - (2 cans) chilled
- 8 c raspberry-flavored ginger -ale,chilled
- 1 fresh mint sprigs -(optional)
- 1 pineapple cubes,(optional)

Combine first 3 ingredients in a small saucepan; bring to a boil.

Reduce heat, and simmer, uncovered, 5 minutes or until candies melt, stirring occasionally. Cool completely.

Combine cinnamon mixture and juice in a large punch bowl; stir well. Add ginger ale; stir gently. Yield 5-1/2 quarts (serving size 1 cup).

REFRESHING PUNCH

➤ CINNAMON TEA PUNCH

Yield 4 Servings

- ❖ 1 c apple juice
- ❖ 1c apricot nectar
- ❖ 1 cinnamon sticks
- ❖ 2 c cinnamon-flavored herb tea
- ❖ 1 ground cinnamon, For Garnish -(opt)

Combine the juice, nectar, and cinnamon sticks in a saucepan and simmer over low heat for 1-2 min, stirring occasionally. Add the tea and stir to mix all the ingredients together. Remove the cinnamon sticks and pour the mixture into 4 mugs; sprinkle with ground cinnamon, if desired.

REFRESHING PUNCH

➤ CITRUS CHAMPAGNE PUNCH

Yield 1 Servings

- ❖ 6 lemons
- ❖ 3 oranges
- ❖ 3 bottles sauternes, 375 ml -each
- ❖ 1 1/2 c creme de cassis, chilled
- ❖ 3/4 c pineapple juice, chilled
- ❖ 2 c strawberries, halved
- ❖ 1 c blueberries, optional

Cut lemons and oranges crosswise in half. Squeeze juice into bowl or large glass measuring cup and pout into 20-24 cup punch bowl.

Add Champagne, Sauternes, cassis, and pineapple juice to punch bowl; stir to combine.

Add strawberries and blueberries if desired to punch.

REFRESHING
PUNCH

➤ CITRUS FRUIT PUNCH

Yield 1 Servings

- ❖ 1 cn orange juice,Frozen -concentrate,thawed (12 oz.
- ❖ 1 cn lemonade concentrate,Frozen - (12 oz.),Thawed
- ❖ 1 cn limeade concentrate,Frozen -thawed (12 oz.)
- ❖ 4 c cold water
- ❖ 1 l ginger ale,chilled \orange,lemon or lime slices - for garnish

In punch bowl or 2 1/2 quart pitcher, combine concentrates and water; mix well. Stir in ginger ale; serve immediately. Garnish with fruit slices, if desired.

Yield twelve (1-cup) servings.

REFRESHING PUNCH

➤ CITRUS MINT PUNCH

Yield 3 Servings

- ❖ 1 c fresh mint leaves,Packed
- ❖ 1 peel of 1 orange,Grated
- ❖ 1 peel of 1 lemon,Grated
- ❖ 3 c water,Boiling
- ❖ 12 oz can lemonade,Frozen --concentrate,thawed
- ❖ 12 oz can orange juice,Frozen --concentrat,e, thawed
- ❖ 1 1/2 qt cold water
- ❖ 1 additional mint leaves(opt.)

Place mint leaves and peels in a heat-resistant pitcher or bowl; add boiling water. Let steep 1 hour; strain. Add concentrates and water; stir well. Chill. Serve over ice; garnish with mint if desired.

REFRESHING PUNCH

➤ CITRUS PUNCH YIELD

Yield 3 Servings

- 1 1/2 c
- sugar
- 3c water
- 1T tea,Instan
- t 1 1/2 c lime juice
- 1 cn (46-oz) blended grapefruit -and oran,ge juice
- 1 ice cubes
- 4 c ginger ale

Combine sugar and water in saucepan; place over low heat and stir until sugar is dissolved. Add to instant tea. Add juices; chill. Pour into punch bowl; add ice cubes; stir until ice is partially melted. Just before serving, add ginger ale. Garnish with lime slices and maraschino cherries.

Yield 44 (1/2-cup) servings.

REFRESHING
PUNCH

➤ CITRUS SPARKLER PUNCH

Yield 2 Servings

- 8 oz bottle lime juice
- 8 oz bottle lemon juice
- 2 liters club soda
- 2 (46 oz) cans unsweetened -pineapple,juice
- 1 qt orange juice
- 2 liters ginger ale
- 2 lemons
- 2 oranges
- 2 c sugar (can use less)

This will fill two punch bowls. Mix first five ingredients together.this can be done ahead of time. When ready pour half of the mixture into a punch bowl. Add one liter of ginger ale and one liter club soda. Add slices of fresh lemon and orange for decoration.

if desired, a mold of the mixture can be frozen the night before to keep the punch cold while not diluting it.

REFRESHING PUNCH

➤ CITRUS TEA PUNCH WITH FRESH MINT

Yield 10 Servings

- ❖ 10 c water,Boiling
- ❖ 6 tea bags
- ❖ 6 whole cloves
- ❖ Zest of 1 lemon,removed in -strips
- ❖ Zest of 1 orange,removed in - strips
- ❖ 2/3 c sugar
- ❖ 1 cn lemonade - (12 oz),Frozen -thawed
- ❖ 2 T mint leaves
- ❖ 10   mint sprigs

Pour boiling water over tea bags, cloves, lemon zest and orange zest. Cover. Let steep 5 minutes.

Use tongs to transfer tea bags to plate (when cool enough to handle, squeeze tea bags over pot to release all tea); stir in sugar until

REFRESHING PUNCH

dissolved. Stir in lemonade. Chill several hours or up to 2 days.

One hour before serving, stir in mint leaves and refrigerate. Strain tea. Put ice cubes in chilled stemmed glasses. Pour in tea; garnish with mint sprig.

REFRESHING PUNCH

➤ CLARENCE MOODY'S HOLIDAY PUNCH

Yield 40 Servings

- 3 pieces ginger
- 1 stick (3) cinnamon
- 8 whole cloves (up to)
- 4 cardamon seeds
- 6 lemons
- 6 sm oranges
- 1 ga apple cider
- 1 qt pineapple juice
- 1/2 t salt

Tie spices in cheesecloth. Peel and cut lemons & oranges into thin slices and add to cider and juice. To this, add spice bag and bring to a low simmering boil. Stir as it simmers for 15 minutes then add salt and stir vigorously. Serve hot.

REFRESHING PUNCH

➤ CLARET PUNCH

Yield 1 Servings

- ❖ 2/3 c sugar
- ❖ 1 qt water
- ❖ 1pt claret
- ❖ 2 lemons,juice of
- ❖ 1ice,Cracked
- ❖ 2 sprigs mint
- ❖ 1 orange
- ❖ 1 a few fresh strawberries,if - in season

Dissolve the sugar in the water; add claret, lemon juice, ice, and mint, crushing the latter slightly to extract its fragrance. Slice the orange thinly and add with the strawberries at the time of serving.

REFRESHING PUNCH

➤ COCA-COLA PUNCH

Yield 25 Servings

- ❖ 12 lemons, juiced
- ❖ 3c sugar
- ❖ 5pt water
- ❖ 6 king size coca-colas

Combine lemon juice, sugar and water. Let stand overnight in refrigerator. When ready to serve add Coca-Colas and ice. Good punch for children.

Yield 25 punch cup servings.

REFRESHING
PUNCH

➤ COCONUT RUM PUNCH

Yield 1 Servings

This is a version of an old recipe from Barbados. You can use light or dark rum. One of the ingredients is simple syrup which is made by dissolving 4 parts (any measure) sugar in 3 parts of water. If you can't find a fresh young coconut, the chilled drinks cabinet in many

Asian food stores contain young coconut juice, which has been frozen in plastic packs.

Put into a cocktail shaker or mixing bowl 30 ml lime juice, 60 ml simple syrup, 90 ml rum. 120 ml young coconut- nut juice. Shake or stir with ice cubes and strain into a tall glass. Garnish with a lime leaf.

Serves 1

REFRESHING PUNCH

➤ COFFEE CHOCOLATE PUNCH

Yield 1 Servings

- ❖ 1/2 c coffee, Instant
- ❖ 2 c hot water
- ❖ 1 c sugar
- ❖ 1 ga milk
- ❖ 1/2 ga chocolate ice cream
- ❖ 1/2 ga vanilla ice cream

In saucepan combine coffee, water and sugar. Bring to boil over med. Heat, stirring frequently. Remove from heat; cool and Pour into punch bowl; stir in milk. Add ice creams; stir until smooth. Serves 50

REFRESHING PUNCH

➤ COFFEE EGGNOG PUNCH

Yield 1 Servings

- 64 oz eggnog, chilled
- 1/4 c light brown sugar, packed
- 1 T coffee, Instant
- 1/4 t cinnamon
- 1/2 c kahlua
- 1/2 c bourbon -or- brandy
- 1 c whipping cream
- 1/4 c powdered sugar
- 1 t vanilla

In large mixer bowl, combine eggnog, brown sugar, coffee and cinnamon; beat on low speed until sugar and coffee are dissolved. Stir in Kahlua and bourbon; chill. In small mixer bowl, beat cream with powdered sugar and vanilla until stiff. Pour eggnog mixture into punch bowl; top with whipped cream. Refrigerate leftovers.

REFRESHING PUNCH

➤ COFFEE MOCHA PUNCH

Yield 10 Servings

- ❖ 1 stephen ceideburg
- ❖ 4 c strong coffee,chilled
- ❖ 1 qt chocolate ice cream
- ❖ 1 qt vanilla ice cream
- ❖ 1 c whipping cream,well-chilled
- ❖ 1/4 t salt
- ❖ 1/2 c granulated sugar
- ❖ 1/4 t almond extract
- ❖ 1/2 t vanilla
- ❖ 1/2 t nutmeg,Ground
- ❖ 1/4 t ground cinnamon,optional

Pour chilled coffee into a punch bowl. Add walnut-sized chunks of ice cream.

Whip cream, adding salt, sugar, almond extract and vanilla. Whip

REFRESHING PUNCH

until soft peaks form. Fold into punch. Sprinkle with nutmeg and optional cinnamon.

Makes 10 servings

REFRESHING PUNCH

➤ COFFEE POT PUNCH

Yield 12 Servings

- 1 1/2 qt cranberry juice
- 2 qt apple juice
- 1/2 c brown sugar, firmly packed
- 1/2 t salt
- 4 cinnamon sticks
- 1 1/2 t cloves, Ground

Pour juices into a 30 cup percolator. Place sugar and spices in the basket. Place basket in the pot and perk. Serve hot in mugs. Serves 12 with enough for seconds.

REFRESHING PUNCH

➤ COFFEE PUNCH

Yield 1 Servings

- ❖ 1 half gal. vanilla ice cream
- ❖ 1 pot of coffee
- ❖ 1 chocolate syrup,(enough to -cover the top

Put the ice cream in a punch bowl, pour chocolate syrup over the top and add the pot of coffee (hot). You can add Baileys or a coffee liqueur.

REFRESHING PUNCH

➤ COFFEE VANILLA PUNCH

Yield 1 Servings

- ❖ 1 qt heavy cream
- ❖ 5 sugar
- ❖ 5 vanilla
- ❖ 2 qt vanilla ice cream
- ❖ 1 ga strong black coffee, well

Whip cream until stiff; beat in sugar and vanilla. Put ice cream and whipped cream in punch bowl. Pour chilled coffee over all. Mix. Serves 50 to 60

REFRESHING PUNCH

➤ COFFEE-KAHLUA PUNCH

Yield 18 Servings

- 8 1/4 c hot strong brewed coffee
- 1/3 c sugar
- 4 c skim milk
- 1 T vanilla extract
- 1 1/4 c Kahlua (or other) -coffee-flavored liq
- 5 c vanilla ice milk, softened
- 1 square semisweet chocolate -(1-ounce) coarsely

Combine coffee and sugar, stirring until sugar dissolves. Stir in milk and vanilla; cover and chill. Combine chilled coffee mixture and Kahlua in a punch bowl; stir well. Spoon tablespoons of ice milk into coffee mixture; stir until ice milk melts. Sprinkle with chocolate. Yield 4-1/2 quarts (serving size 1 cup).

REFRESHING PUNCH

➤ COLD KAHLUA COFFEE PUNCH

Yield 48 Servings

- 6 oz dry
- coffee,Instant
- 1 1/2 c sugar
- 1qt water,boiling
- 1ga vanilla ice cream
- 2 c kahlua
- 2 qt milk
- 2 qt water,cold

Dissolve coffee and sugar in 1 quart boiling water; stir well and refrigerate. When ready to serve, combine cold coffee mix with the remaining ingredients and pour into a punch bowl. Leave the ice cream in one large chunk. Serve in punch cups.

REFRESHING
PUNCH

➤COLLEGE PUNCH YIELD

10 Servings

- ❖ 2 qt pineapple juice
- ❖ 2 qt apple juice
- ❖ 2 qt orange juice 1 qt ginger ale
- ❖ 1 qt orange sherbet
- ❖ 1 strawberries, For Garnish

Combine and mix all ingredients in container; serve

REFRESHING PUNCH

➤ CORAL PUNCH

Yield 1 Servings

- ❖ 1 cn Pineapple Juice,(46 oz. -each)
- ❖ 2 qt Lemonade
- ❖ 1 1/2 qt Orange Juice
- ❖ 1qt Cranberry Juice Cocktail
- ❖ 2 c Apple Juice
- ❖ 2 l Ginger Ale

REFRESHING PUNCH

➤ COWBOY PUNCH YIELD

10 Servings

- ❖ 2 l White Grape Juice
- ❖ 1 l Club Soda
- ❖ 2 l 7-Up

Mix the ingredients. Chill thoroughly. Serve very well chilled. Tastes like Champagne.

REFRESHING PUNCH

➤ CRAN-ORANGE PUNCH

Yield 8 Servings

- ❖ 1 1/4 c cranberry juice -reduced-calorie
- ❖ 6 oz (1) cn orange juice -unsweetened concen,Frozen
- ❖ 2c diet lemon-line soda
- ❖ 1sugar subsitute to equal
- ❖ 1/4 c sugar

Combine cranberry juice, orange concentrate, and sugar substitute in a large bowl; stir well and chill. Add soda to fruit juice mixture just before serving. Serve over crushed ice.

REFRESHING PUNCH

➤CRANBERRY HOLIDAY PUNCH

Yield 1 Servings

- ❖ 1 qt ginger ale
- ❖ 1 qt orange soda
- ❖ 8 oz lemon-lime soda
- ❖ 2 c cranberry juice cocktail

Freeze one quart ginger ale for beverage cubes. When ready to serve, pour cranberry juice, sodas and the remaining 1 qt. ginger ale into punch bowl.

Float beverage cubes in punch. Can garnish with orange slices and mint leaves. Serves 24 punch-size cups.

REFRESHING
PUNCH

➤ CRANBERRY LEMON PUNCH

Yield 1 Servings

- ❖ 1 pk lemonade drink mix (2-quart -size)
- ❖ 5 c cold water
- ❖ 1 bottle (32 oz) cranberry -juice cock,tail, chilled
- ❖ 3/4 c vodka,optional
- ❖ 1 lemon and orange,Slices -optional
- ❖ 1 ice

In large pitcher, add drink mix then water; stir to dissolve. Add cranberry juice and vodka, if desired. Garnish with lemon and orange slices if desired.

REFRESHING PUNCH

➤ CRANBERRY LIME NONALCOHOLIC PUNCH

Yield 28 Servings

- ❖ 1 cranberry cocktail bottle
- ❖ 2 c limeade concentrate, Frozen
- ❖ 2 c pineapple juice
- ❖ 2 ginger ale bottles, 300 ml
- ❖ 2 soda water bottles, 750 ml -ice

In punch bowl, combine cranberry cocktail, limeade concentrate, pineapple and ginger ale. Just before serving, add soda water and ice.

REFRESHING PUNCH

➤ CRANBERRY ORANGE PUNCH

Yield 1 Servings

- ❖ 2 bottles (32-ounce) cranberry - juice,cocktail, chilled
- ❖ 1 1/2 c realemon,(r) lemon juice -from conc 2/3 c sugar
- ❖ 2 cn (12-ounce) orange soda -chilled ice

In large punch bowl, combine cranberry juice, REALEMON(r) brand and sugar; stir until sugar dissolves. Just before serving, add orange soda and ice. Garnish as desired.

REFRESHING PUNCH

➤ CRANBERRY ORANGE TEA PUNCH

Yield 15 Servings

- 1 1/2 c cranberries
- 1 lemon,thinly sliced -crosswise
- 1 1/2 qt cranberry juice
- 1 1/2 c sugar
- 2 c apple juice,chilled
- 1/2 c plus 2 tablespoons freshly -squeeze,d lemon juice chi
- 1 c orange juice,chilled
- 1c strong orange pekoe tea -chilled
- 2 c club soda,chilled
- 1white rum,to taste
- 2 sm oranges,thinly sliced -crosswise

1) In a medium ring mold, combine cranberries and lemon slices. Pour enough cranberry juice over them to fill mold, about 2 to 3 cups.

REFRESHING
PUNCH

Freeze.

2) In a medium pan, combine sugar with 1 1/2 quarts water. Bring to a boil, then turn off heat and let cool completely. Chill.

3) In a punch bowl, combine sugar syrup, apple juice, lemon juice, orange juice, tea and club soda. Add white rum to taste. Unmold ice ring into punch. To serve, fill tall glasses with ice. Place an orange slice in each glass and ladle punch over it. Yield about 15 servings.

REFRESHING PUNCH

➤ CRANBERRY PARTY PUNCH

Yield 1 Servings

- 1 cn (12 oz.) lemonade, Frozen
- 1 and diluted, Thawed
- 1 qt cranberry juice cocktail
- 1 c orange juice, Frozen
- 1 and undiluted, Thawed
- 1 bottle of ginger ale (28 oz)
- 1 orange, thinly sliced

Combine juices and chill. Add ginger ale just before serving.

Garnish with orange slices. Yields 1.5 gallons. One of the cans of lemonade concentrate may be diluted and frozen to make an ice ring or cubes.

REFRESHING PUNCH

➤ CRANBERRY VODKA PUNCH

Yield 15 Servings

- ❖ 1/2 qt vodka
- ❖ 1 1/2 qt cranberry juice (48 oz.)
- ❖ 3/4 qt orange juice (24 oz.)
- ❖ 3/4 qt pineapple juice (24 oz.)

Mix all ingredients together. If you wish, you can add as much ginger ale as you want. This looks very nice with a frozen ring made with one part cranberry juice, 1/2 part orange juice, and 1/2 part pineapple juice.

REFRESHING PUNCH

➤ CRANBERRY ZINFANDEL PUNCH

Yield 1 Servings

- 1 64 -ounce bottle -cranberry-juice cocktail,c
- 1 750 -milliliter bottle red
- -zinfandel wine,chilled
- 1/3 c bottled sweetened lime juice
- 1 1 liter bottle seltzer
- chilled lime for,Slices -garnish

In large pitcher or punch bowl (about 5 quarts), mix cranberry-juice cocktail, Zinfandel, and lime juice. Refrigerate until ready to serve. Just before serving, stir in seltzer; garnish with lime slices.

REFRESHING PUNCH

➤ CRANBERRY-CIDER PUNCH

Yield 32 Servings

- ❖ 2 l cranberry ginger ale
- ❖ 1 chilled
- ❖ 2 l apple cider, chilled
- ❖ 3 limes
- ❖ 1 cn (341ml) raspberry, Frozen
- ❖ 1 juice concentrate, optional

Pour ginger ale and cider into punch bowl. Squeeze juice from 2 of the limes and thinly slice the third. Stir juice into punch. Taste and add raspberry concentrate, if you wish. If concentrate is still frozen, you may not need to add ice. Refrigerate until serving time. Float lime slices on surface. Makes 16 cups, enough for 32 punch-glass servings.

REFRESHING PUNCH

➤ CRANBERRY-LEMON PUNCH

Yield 1 Servings

- ❖ 1 1/2 qt water
- ❖ 1 c sugar
- ❖ 1 c strong tea
- ❖ 1 6oz.can lemonade, Frozen
- ❖ 1 concentrate, thawed
- ❖ 1 qt cranberry juice cocktail
- ❖ 2 c apple juice
- ❖ 1 c orange juice

Heat water and sugar to boiling, stirring constantly, until sugar is dissolved; cool. Prepare tea, using 2 teaspoons loose tea or 2 tea bags and 1 cup boiling water; cool. Refrigerate all ingredients. Just before serving, mix in large punch bowl.

To make ice ring, arrange thin citrus slices and cranberries in 6 cup ring mold. Pour water into mold to partially cover fruit. Freeze. When frozen, add water to fill mold 3/4 full. Freeze. Unmold and float fruit side up in punch bowl. Makes about 30 servings, ½ cup each.

REFRESHING PUNCH

➤ CRANBERRY-PEACH PUNCH

Yield 4 Servings

- ❖ 1 1/2 c water
- ❖ 2 cinnamon sticks
- ❖ 2 bags peach-flavored tea
- ❖ 1 T lime juice
- ❖ 1 T honey (or), To Taste
- ❖ 2 c cranberry (or lingonberry) -juice

Bring the water to a boil in a large pan with the cinnamon sticks and tea bags. Remove the pan from the heat and let the tea steep for 10 minutes. Remove the tea bags and cinnamon sticks. Stir in the lime juice, honey and cranberry juice. Transfer the mixture to a pitcher and chill.

REFRESHING PUNCH

➤ CRANBERRY-WINE PUNCH

Yield 3 Servings

- ❖ 1 1/2 qt cranberry juice cocktail -chilled
- ❖ 4 c burgundy (or other dry red) -wine,chilled
- ❖ 2 c unsweetened orange juice -chilled
- ❖ 1 orange slices,(optional)

Combine first 3 ingredients in a large bowl; stir well. Yield 3 quarts

REFRESHING
PUNCH

➤ CRANBERRY/RASPBERRY PUNCH

Yield 50 Servings

- ❖ 3 1/2 ga raspberry sherbet
- ❖ 2 1/2 qt vanilla ice cream
- ❖ 2 qt cranberry cocktail
- ❖ 2 qt sprite

Soften sherbet and ice cream. Add 1 qt. of juice; mix. Add remaining juice; blend well. Just before serving, add Sprite.

REFRESHING PUNCH

➤ CREAMY PINEAPPLE PUNCH

Yield 1 Servings

- ❖ 1 cn pineapple juice,chilled (46 - oz.)
- ❖ 1 1/2 pt vanilla ice cream,softened
- ❖ 1 pt orange sherbet,softened
- ❖ 3 c ginger ale,chilled

In large bowl, combine pineapple juice, ice cream and sherbet; stir until blended. Pour into punch bowl. Add ginger ale. Serve immediately. Yield eighteen (3/4-cup) servings.

REFRESHING PUNCH

➤ CREAMY PUNCH YIELD

6 Servings

- ❖ 1/2 ga vanilla ice cream
- ❖ 1/2 ga rainbow sherbet
- ❖ 1 lg can pineapple juice
- ❖ 2 l sprite (or 7-up)

Mash ice cream and sherbet together in punch bowl. Add pineapple juice and soda.

REFRESHING PUNCH

➤ CREOLE COFFEE ICE CREAM PUNCH

Yield 12 Servings

- ❖ 6 eggs
- ❖ 1/2 c sugar
- ❖ 3 c louisiana coffee w/chicory
- ❖ 1/4 c bourbon
- ❖ 1/2 pt vanilla ice cream
- ❖ 1/2 pt coffee ice cream

1) In large bowl, beat eggs at high speed until slightly thickened.

2) Gradually add sugar, beating until mixture is smooth and very thick.

3) Add coffee and bourbon; mix thoroughly.

4) Pour mixture into punch bowl or large pitcher.

5) Spoon in ice cream; stir well. Allow ice cream to melt slightly to flavor punch, then serve immediately.

REFRESHING
PUNCH

➤ CROCKED PUNCH

Yield 12 Servings

- 3 cn water
- 5 whole cloves
- 2 cinnamon sticks
- 1 t nutmeg,Ground
- 3/4 t ginger,Ground
- 1 sm can fozen orange juice -concentrate
- 1qt apple cider
- 1orange,Slices

In a slow cooker heat water and spices on high for 30-60 minutes.

Remove cloves and cinnamon sticks. Add orange juice concentrate and apple cider. Heat but do not boil. Garnish with orange slices. Serves 12-15.

REFRESHING PUNCH

➤ DAIQUIRI PUNCH YIELD

4 Servings

- ❖ 1/2 c light corn syrup
- ❖ 2 c light rum
- ❖ 1cn (6 oz. each) daiquiri,Frozen - mix,thawed
- ❖ 2bottles (28oz) each)
- ❖ -carbonated wat,er, chilled
- ❖ 1 ice ring
- ❖ 1lime,cut into thin slices

Mix corn syrup and rum in punch bowl stirring to blend. Stir in daiquiri mix.

Just before serving add carbonated water then carefully slide in ice ring and add lime. Makes about 25 - 4 ounce servings.

REFRESHING PUNCH

➤ DEES' VODKA PUNCH

Yield 1 Servings

- ❖ 1 pk (3 oz.) of strawberry jello
- ❖ 2 c water, Boiling
- ❖ 1 cn (46 oz.) orange juice
- ❖ 1cn (46 oz.) pineapple juice
- ❖ 1 c lemon juice
- ❖ 2 c vodka
- ❖ 1 bottle,(33.8 oz) gingerale
- ❖ 1/2 ga sherbet

DISSOLVE JELLO IN THE BOILING WATER AND LET IT COOL TO ROOM TEMPERATURE THEN ADD THE INGREDIENTS LISTED ABOVE, IN THE ORDER THEY ARE LISTED.

REFRESHING PUNCH

➤ DELICIOUS COFFEE PUNCH

Yield 50 Servings

- ❖ 4 qt strong coffee
- ❖ 5 5 t vanilla
- ❖ 6 T sugar
- ❖ 1 qt whipping cream, whipped and -chilled
- ❖ 2 qt (or more) vanilla ice cream

Prepare coffee. Add vanilla and sugar. Chill. Before serving, spoon ice cream into punch bowl. Add coffee mixture and fold in whipped cream. Mix well. Taste before serving and add more sugar, if needed. Yield 50 servings.

REFRESHING
PUNCH

➤ DELICIOUS PARTY PUNCH

Yield 1 Servings

- 1 pk (large) drink mix, any -flavor
- 2 qt water
- 2 c pineapple juice
- 3/4 c sugar
- 1/4 c lemon juice
- 1   sherbet, any flavor

Combine all ingredients & freeze until slushy. Pour over any flavor sherbet 10 minutes before serving. Makes 1-1/2 gallons.

REFRESHING PUNCH

➤ DELICIOUS SUMMER PUNCH

Yield 1 Servings

- 1 cn (12-oz) orange juice,Frozen -concent,rate (thawed)
- 1cn (6-oz) lemonade,Frozen -(thawed)
- 1bottle (32-oz) cranberry -juice cock,tail, chilled
- 1bottle (2-litre) sprite

Add juices to the punchbowl and stir. Then SLOWLY pour in Sprite.

REFRESHING PUNCH

➤ DELORES'S PUNCH

Yield 80 Servings

- ❖ 1 sm box jello (or 1 large.)
- ❖ 2 3 c sugar
- ❖ 2 qt hot water
- ❖ 3/4 c real lemon
- ❖ 1/2 cn large pineapple juice
- ❖ 1 sm orange, Frozen
- ❖ 1 concentrate 2 qt cold water
- ❖ 2 bottles favorite pop

Add jello (any flavor), 3 cups sugar and 2 quarts hot water, stir until dissolved. Add 3/4 cup Real Lemon, 1/2 of large can Pineapple juice, 1 small can frozen orange juice concentrate and 2 quarts cold water, then freeze. Let thaw just prior to serving and mash with a hand potatoe masher or something until a slush. Add 2 bottles 7up, sprite, mountain dew or what ever you have. Makes 7 quarts or 80 servings..

REFRESHING PUNCH

➤ DESMOND'S RUM PUNCH

Yield 1 Servings

- 1 oz lime juice, freshly squeezed
- 2 oz sugar syrup, recipe follows
- 1 oz over-proof white rum
- 2 oz dark rum
- 2 dr angostura bitters
- 1 c ice, Crushed
- 1 fresh sugarcane swizzle -stick
- SUGAR SYRUP
- 1/2 c sugar
- 1/4 c water

Combine all ingredients in a large cocktail shaker. Shake well to combine. Pour into a glass. Garnish with swizzle stick.

SUGAR SYRUP Makes 3/4 cup

Combine sugar and water in a small saucepan. Boil for 5 minutes. Let cool. Store extra syrup in refrigerator, and use as needed.

REFRESHING PUNCH

➤ DISHWATER PUNCH

Yield 50 Servings

- ❖ 1 cn pineapple juice
- ❖ 1/2 qt apple juice
- ❖ 1 pk grape koolaid
- ❖ 2 pk tuttifruiti koolaid
- ❖ 1 pk tropical punch koolaid
- ❖ 1 1/2 pk strawberry koolaid
- ❖ 11 qt water
- ❖ 1 red food color

Make sure all koolaid is *pre-sweetened* 2-quart packages. Mix all dry mixes together. Add water and juices. stir well. Add food color until it looks drinkable. Without any food color, it should look like its name. Depending on how sensitive your guests are, you may need LOTS of food color (we have used up to a whole BIG bottle).

REFRESHING PUNCH

➤ DOTS PUNCH YIELD

50 Servings

- ❖ 12 oz orange juice, Frozen -concentrate
- ❖ 6 oz lemonade, frozen concentrate
- ❖ 18 oz pineapple juice
- ❖ 6 c water
- ❖ 6 pt cranberry juice cocktail

Add water to frozen concetrate as directed on cans. Mix all ingredients well.

Serve in punchbowl over ice.

Make ice cubes by putting red and green cherries in cubes. freezes very well.

REFRESHING PUNCH

➤ DOUBLE SHERBET PUNCH

Yield 1 Servings

- ❖ 12 oz orange juice,frozen,-concentrate
- ❖ 6 oz lemonade,frozen concentrate
- ❖ 3 c pineapple juice
- ❖ 1 qt lime sherbet
- ❖ 1 1/2 qt ginger ale,chilled

Mix orange juice and lemonade as directed on lable.

combine orange, lemonade and pineapple juce. Refrigerate 2 hours or until serving time.

When ready to serve, pour juice mixture into punch bowl, add sherbet to punch in small scoops. Add ginger ale.

REFRESHING PUNCH

➤ DREAMSICLE PUNCH

Yield 1 Servings

- ❖ 1 cn orange juice, frozen
- ❖ 1 concentrate
- ❖ 1 cn light rum
- ❖ 2 scoops ice, Crushed
- ❖ 2 l a&w cream soda
- ❖ 1 T vanilla extract -- (the real
- ❖ 1 stuff)

Put the OJ Concentrate and 1 measure of alcohol (use the concentrate can for the measure) and vanilla in a big sealable container (an old water jug works nicely.) Shake it up until it is well mixed. Then place this goop in the freezer until slushy. Once slushy, add a couple scoops of crushed ice and shake again until mixed. Slowly add the A&Ws. now stir or just turn the jug up and down a few times to mix. DO NOT SHAKE hard. It is now ready to serve. Keep covered so it doesn't lose carbonation.

REFRESHING PUNCH

➤ DUDLEY EPPEL'S HOT CIDER-CRANBERRY PUNCH

Yield 12 Servings

- ❖ 8 c apple cider
- ❖ 4c cranberry juice cocktail
- ❖ 3cinnamon sticks
- ❖ 4 cloves, whole
- ❖ 3 strips orange peel
- ❖ 1 c dark rum

1) Put cider, cranberry juice, cinnamon, cloves and orange peel into a large pot. Bring to a boil over medium-high heat. Reduce heat and simmer, uncovered 25 to 35 minutes.

2) Line a strainer with cheesecloth and strian punch. Put 1 to 2 tablespoons of rum into each mug, then fill to the rim with hot punch.

REFRESHING PUNCH

➤ EASY PARTY PUNCH

Yield 16 Servings

- ❖ 1 46 ounce can unsweetened
- ❖ -pineapple juice
- ❖ 1 46 ounce can apple juice
- ❖ 2 28 oz bottle
- ❖ 7-up, chilled (1 - 2 liter works fine)

Freeze juices in the cans. Remove juice from freezer 1 hour in advance, or sit cans in a sink of warm water for 10- 15 minutes. It should be slushy. Mix up in large punch bowl and serve.

REFRESHING PUNCH

➤ EASY PUNCH YIELD

12 Servings

- ❖ 1 cn (46-oz) unsweetened -pineapple juice
- ❖ 1 qt ginger ale
- ❖ 1 ice ring, cherries and/or -strawberry

Chill all ingredients before mixing. Mix only as needed. Decorate with ice ring or fresh mint leaves. Serves 12 to 16.

REFRESHING PUNCH

➤ ELLY MAY'S WEDDING PUNCH

Yield 1 Servings

- ❖ 1 3 oz pkg cherry gelatin
- ❖ 9 c water, Boiling
- ❖ 4 c sugar
- ❖ 4 c water
- ❖ 2 46 oz can pineapple juice
- ❖ 6 oz orange juice, Frozen
- ❖ 4 T lemon juice
- ❖ 1 2 l bottle ginger ale

Dissolve the gelatin in the boiling water in a large saucepan. In a separate saucepan boil together the sugar and 4 cups water. Add the pineapple juice, orange juice and lemon juice. Cool. Combine the gelatin and juice mixtures. Pour into plastic containers and freeze.

Set out about 3 hours before serving. Add the ginger ale just before serving. The punch will be slushy.

REFRESHING PUNCH

➤ EMERIL'S FROZEN MILK PUNCH 1

- 1/4 c brandy
- 1 1/4 c bourbon
- 1 1/4 c dark rum
- 3 qt half-and-half
- 4 T pure Mexican vanilla
- 3/4 c simple syrup - (to 1 cup)-equal parts sugar and water, simmered til -sugar dissolves
- Freshly-grated nutmeg, to -taste

In a plastic gallon container, with a lid, combine the brandy, bourbon, rum, half-and-half, and vanilla. Mix well. Sweeten the cream mixture to taste with the simple syrup. Cover and freeze until slightly frozen.

To serve, using an ice pick, slush the mixture. Spoon into balloon wine glasses and garnish with nutmeg.

This recipe yields 4 quarts.

REFRESHING PUNCH

➤ ERDBEER BOWLE (STRAWBERRY WINE PUNCH)

Yield 1 Servings

- ❖ 1/2 pt strawberries, stemless,
- ❖ 1 rinsed, cut in half
- ❖ 1 T granulated sugar
- ❖ ½ bottle german riesling, well
- ❖ 1 chilled
- ❖ 1 T brandy (preferably alsbach
- ❖ 1 uralt)
- ❖ ½ bottle german sekt well
- ❖ 1 chilled

Place the strawberries in a large covered glass jar (a sun tea jar will be fine), sprinkle them with sugar and drizzle them with the brandy. Set them aside to marinate for two hours to allow the sugar to draw out the juice from the berries. Add white wine, stir, and set aside for two additional hours. When ready to serve, pour in serving punch

REFRESHING PUNCH

bowl. Add Sekt and serve chilled in wide champagne type glasses, making sure to distribute strawberries with the wine.

serves 4

REFRESHING PUNCH

➤ EVERGREEN MINT PUNCH

Yield 1 Servings

- ❖ 1 1/2 c water
- ❖ 10 oz mint jelly
- ❖ 3 c pineapple juice, chilled
- ❖ 1/2 c lemon juice
- ❖ 1 1/2 c vodka
- ❖ 64 oz lemon-lime carbonated drink - chilled
- ❖ 1 qt lime sherbet

In small saucepan, combine water and jelly; cook and stir until jelly melts. Cool. In large punch bowl, combine jelly mix, juices and vodka. Just before serving, add carbonated beverage and lime sherbet.

REFRESHING PUNCH

➤ EYE OPENERS - MILK PUNCH

Yield 1 Servings

- ❖ 1 1/2 oz randy
- ❖ 1/2 t anilla extract
- ❖ 1/2 oz imple syrup
- ❖ 1 oz alf and half
- ❖ 2 oz ilk
- ❖ F reshly-grated nutmeg

In a cocktail shaker combine brandy, vanilla, syrup, half-and-half, and milk; fill with ice cubes. Shake vigorously until chilled; strain into a cocktail glass, dust with nutmeg and serve.

This recipe yields 1 eye opener.

REFRESHING PUNCH

➤ FABULOUS FRUIT PUNCH

Yield 1 Servings

- ❖ 1 cn (48-oz) unsweetened -pineapple juice
- ❖ 1 c sweetened orange juice
- ❖ 1/4 c fresh lime juice
- ❖ 1/2 c fresh lemon juice
- ❖ 1/3 c loosely-packed mint leaves
- ❖ 1 bottle soda water
- ❖ 1c fresh strawberries,halved
- ❖ 1unpeeled lemon,Sliced

Combine fruit juices and mint in pitcher or plastic container. Chill at least two hours. Remove mint leaves with slotted spoon or strainer. Pour into punch bowl over ice cubes. Gently add soda water. Float strawberries and lemon slices on top.

REFRESHING PUNCH

➤ FABULOUS PUNCH (NO SUGAR)

Yield 18 Servings

- ❖ 1 pk Jell-O Gelatin Sugarfree -'Small Pkg,Strawberry
- ❖ 2 c hot water
- ❖ 1/2 c fresh lemon juice
- ❖ 2 c pineapple juice
- ❖ 6 Bananas,Ripe, Mashed
- ❖ 12 pk Equal. Sweetener
- ❖ 6 c cold water
- ❖ 2 l Sugar Free 7-up,Or Diet -Ginger Ale

Dissolve Jell-O in hot water. Mash bananas in the bowl, Add Jello Mixture, Add remaining ingredients, except 7-up. Add Chilled 7-Up just before serving.

REFRESHING PUNCH

➤ FALL PUNCH YIELD

1 Servings

- ❖ 8 sm apples
- ❖ 8 c water
- ❖ 2 cn apple juice,Frozen -concentrate,thawed (18 oz)
- ❖ 1 cn orange juice,Frozen
- ❖ -concentrate,thawed (18 oz)
- ❖ 1 cn apricot nectar,(11 1/8 oz)
- ❖ 1cn lemonade concentrate,Frozen - (8 oz),Thawed
- ❖ 1c brown sugar,Firmly Packed
- ❖ 15 whole cloves
- ❖ 6sticks cinnamon
- ❖ 3c white grape juice (or sweet)
- ❖ 1white wine,such as a -reisling

Peel top third of each apple. Place apples in a shallow baking dish. Pour water to a depth of one- half inch into dish around apples. Bake,

REFRESHING
PUNCH

uncovered, at 350 degrees for 50 minutes or until apples are slightly tender, basting occasionally with water. Remove apples from dish and set aside. Combine 8 cups water and remaining ingredients, except grape juice or wine, in a Dutch oven. Bring to a boil, reduce heat and simmer 30 minutes, uncovered. Remove cloves and cinnamon sticks. Stir in wine or grape juice. Serve warm in punch bowl. Float baked apples in punch. Yield 3/4 quarts.

REFRESHING
PUNCH

➤ PUNCH

Yield 1 Servings

COOK UP A MESS OF RHUBARB WITH SOME WATER. STRAIN OFF TO GET THE PRETTY PINK JUICE SAVE A FEW LARGE PIECES AND BITS OF RHUBARB TO FLOAT IN IT ADD SUGAR AND MORE WATER (OR GINGER ALE) TO TASTE - TART TANGY AND IS A GOOD THIRST QUENCHER IF YOU DON'T MAKE IT TOO SWEET

REFRESHING PUNCH

➤ FELINE PUNCH

Yield 1 Servings

- ❖ 1 bottles (1-quart)
- ❖ -cranberry-apple d,rink
- ❖ 1 c brown sugar
- ❖ 1 bottle (1-quart) ginger ale
- ❖ 2 whole oranges
- ❖ 1 whole cloves

Heat the cranberry-apple drink and sugar in a pan until the sugar is dissolved. Let cool thoroughly. When ready to serve, pour into a punch bowl and add the ginger ale.

Create faces on the oranges by studding them with whole cloves to form eyes, noses, and mouths. Place in the punch. Add ice cubes just before serving.

MAKES 24 1/2-cup servings

REFRESHING PUNCH

➤ FESTIVE PUNCH YIELD

50 ervings

- 1cn (large) pineapple juice
- 2 cn (large) apricot-orange juice
- 1 qt apple juice
- 2 qt ginger ale
- 1 qt orange sherbet

1) Combine fruit juices and ginger ale in punch bowl.

2) Float sherbet in punch.

Makes 50 servings.

REFRESHING PUNCH

➤ FIRECRACKER PUNCH

Yield 30 Servings

- ❖ 4 c cranberry juice
- ❖ 1 1/2 c sugar
- ❖ 4 c pineapple juice
- ❖ 1 T almond extract
- ❖ 2 qt ginger ale

Combine first 4 ingredients; stir until sugar is dissolved. Chill. Add ginger ale just before serving. Yield 30

REFRESHING PUNCH

➤ FIRESIDE PUNCH YIELD

12 Servings

- ❖ 6c apple cider
- ❖ 12z can lemonade,Frozen -concentrate
- ❖ 1c granulated sugar
- ❖ 1 c peach schnapps
- ❖ 1 c rum

In a Dutch oven, combine first 3 ingredients, bring to a boil. Remove from heat; stir in schnapps and rum. Serve hot.

Yield 12 - 6 oz. servings.

REFRESHING PUNCH

➤ FISH HOUSE PUNCH

Yield 3 Servings

- ❖ 1 c lemon juice
- ❖ 6 oz super fine sugar
- ❖ 1 1/2 l jamaica gold
- ❖ rum 750 ml cognac
- ❖ 1 c peach brandy
- ❖ 1 block ice
- ❖ 1 pt club soda,chilled
- ❖ 8 qt punch bowl,chilled

Combine lemon juice and sugar in a mixing bowl. Stir until sugar is dissolved. In a 4 quart container, combine lemon juice and sugar mixture, rum, Cognac, peach brandy; stir. Store in refrigerator until chilled, ideally overnight.

REFRESHING PUNCH

➤ FIVE FRUIT PUNCH

Yield 1 Servings

- ❖ 1 bottle (48 ounce)
- ❖ -cranberry-raspberry drink
- ❖ 1 cn frozen -pineapple-orange-guava juic
- ❖ 1 bottle (1 liter) chilled -gingerale
- ❖ 1 bottle champagne,chilled -(get the most i,nexpensive

*(if you can't find that combination, just get pineapple-orange frozen concentrate then find guava juice usually in the Mexican section of the store)

Mix cran-raspberry drink and juice concentrate-refrigerate until time to serve. Just before serving, pour into your punch bowl, add gingerale and champagne. Stir gently. This punch is good served with frozen juice ice cubes or a pretty juice fruit ring.

Fruit Ice Cubes

Fill an ice cube tray with some of the fruit juice-put a cherry or raspberry or a pineapple chunk in the juice and freeze. After they are

REFRESHING
PUNCH

frozen add to the punch and it will not get watered down.

Makes about 28 1/2 cup servings.

# REFRESHING
PUNCH

➤ FLAVOR-PACKED FRUIT PUNCH

Yield 1 Servings

- ❖ 1 cn orange juice,Frozen-concentrate,thawed (12 oun 2 c pineapple juice
- ❖ 2 cn lemon-lime flavored soda (12 ounces each)
- ❖ 12 ice cubes (or one 1-quart-ice)- mold

In a punch bowl or large container, combine the orange juice concentrate and pineapple juice. If not serving right away, cover and refrigerate. Just before serving, add the soda and ice cubes or ice mold.

NOTE You can use flavored ice cubes and almost any flavor fruiit juice.

REFRESHING PUNCH

➤ FRESH FRUIT PUNCH

Yield 12 Servings

- ❖ 2 c Sugar
- ❖ 1 c Water
- ❖ 1 bottle Dry white wine
- ❖ 1 bottle Sparkling water --(1.5 liters)
- ❖ 6 c seeded watermelon,Chopped
- ❖ 1 c mango (or papaya),Chopped
- ❖ 1 c pineapple,Chopped

Combine the sugar and water in a saucepan. Bring to a boil and simmer, stirring occasionally, until the syrup is clear. Set aside to cool. Combine the syrup, wine, and sparkling water and stir well. Add the remaining fruit and serve cold.

This recipe yields 12 to 16 servings.

REFRESHING PUNCH

➤ FROSTED FRUIT PUNCH

Yield 8 Servings

- ❖ 1/2 c sugar
- ❖ 1/2 c water
- ❖ 1 cinnamon stick
- ❖ 3 whole cloves
- ❖ 2 c sauterne
- ❖ 12 oz apple juice
- ❖ 1 c orange juice
- ❖ 1/4 c lemon juice
- ❖ 1 orange sherbet

Combine sugar, water, cinnamon and cloves. Bring to a boil, reduce heat and simmer, uncovered, for 5 minutes. Strain and cool. Mix all remaining ingredients except sherbet, with cinnamon mix. Chill well.

Serve in glass topped with a spoonful of orange sherbet.

REFRESHING PUNCH

➤ FROSTY PINK PUNCH

Yield 3 Servings

- ❖ 1/2 c fine granulated sugar
- ❖ 1/2 c lemon juice
- ❖ 1 pt raspberry sherbet
- ❖ 1 c orange juice
- ❖ 2 c cranberry juice cocktail
- ❖ 28 oz ginger ale, chilled

Combine first four ingredients in punch bowl or large pitcher and stir until sugar is dissolved. Spoon in sherbet. Pour ginger ale over all. Serve with ice (if desired).

REFRESHING PUNCH

➤ FROZEN PUNCH

Yield 3 Servings

- ❖ 4 lg cans orange juice
- ❖ 4lg cans pineapple juice
- ❖ 1lg can of pineapple, Crushed
- ❖ ½ bottle of realemon
- ❖ 2 c water
- ❖ 1 1/4 lb sugar
- ❖ 1 ga orange sherbet
- ❖ 4 bottles of 7 up

Mix juices in very large container, add pineapple. Cook water and sugar until dissolved add to juice. Stir well and freeze. To serve thaw to slush consistency, add sherbet and 7 Up and whip.

REFRESHING PUNCH

➤ FROZEN RUM PUNCH

Yield 1 Servings

- ❖ 2 cn (12-oz) lemonade, Frozen
- ❖ 2 cn (12-oz) orange juice, Frozen
- ❖ 48 oz water
- ❖ 1 pt light rum
- ❖ 1 ginger ale

Empty juices into a very large bowl. Fill each can with water (this provides the 48 oz water called for). Mix well. Add rum & mix well again. Pour into 2 plastic pitchers or bowls with covers. Freeze. Will take 24- 48 hours to freeze hard. When ready to serve, fill glasses about 3/4 full with frozen mixture. Pour ginger ale over this to fill glass. Stir. Will be slushy. Very good summertime drink.

REFRESHING
PUNCH

➤ FRUIT JUICE PUNCH

Yield 50 Servings

- ❖ 3 c sugar
- ❖ 3 qt water
- ❖ 1 c strong tea
- ❖ 12 lemons, juice of
- ❖ 12 oranges, juice of
- ❖ 4 c grape juice
- ❖ 1 cn (8-oz) pineapple, Crushed
- ❖ 8 c ginger ale

Boil sugar and water 8 minutes. Chill; add tea, juices, and pineapple. Set in refrigerator to mellow. Just before serving, add the ginger ale.

Yield 50 servings.

REFRESHING PUNCH

➤ FRUIT MEDLEY PUNCH

Yield 12 Servings

- 1 della robbia ice ring *
- 20 oz (2 pk) strawberries**,Frozen
- 3 c apricot nectar,chilled
- 3 c cold water
- 1 c lemon juice
- 6 oz orange juicethawed***,Frozen
- 1 c sugar
- 32 oz bottle ginger ale,chilled

Ice Ring is optional ** Strawberries are to be the ones frozen in syrup and they should be partially thawed. *** Frozen Orange Juice should be thawed and no water added. Should be concentrate form.

REFRESHING PUNCH

➤ FRUIT MEDLEY PUNCH WITH DELLA ROBBIA ICE RING

Yield 12 Servings

- ❖ 2 pk (10 oz) strawberries,Frozen -in syru,p, thawed
- ❖ 3 c apricot nectar,chilled
- ❖ 3 c cold water
- ❖ 1 c lemon juice
- ❖ 1 cn (6 oz) orange juice,Frozen -concentr,ate, thawed
- ❖ 1 c sugar
- ❖ 1 l bottle ginger ale,chilled
- ❖ for della robbi 2 1/2 c ginger ale,chilled
- ❖ 1/2 c lemon juice
- ❖ 1 assorted fruits*

Use any of the following canned apricot halves, drained; seedless white grapes; strips of orange peel, curled; whole strawberries; mint leaves; drained maraschino cherries.

REFRESHING PUNCH

To make punch Prepare ice ring in advance. In a blender container, blend strawberries well (about 30 seconds). In a large punch bowl, combine strawberries, apricot nectar, water, lemon juice, orange juice concentrate and sugar. Stir until sugar dissolves. Slowly pour in ginger ale. Add ice ring. Makes about 3 1/2 quarts.

To make ice ring In a 1-quart measure or container, combine ginger ale and lemon juice. Pour 1/2 of the mixture into a 1-quart ring mold; arrange fruits, peel and mint leaves in mold. Freeze. Pour remaining liquid over fruit in mold. Freeze.

REFRESHING PUNCH

➤ FRUIT PUNCH YIELD

8 Servings

- ❖ 1qt strawberries
- ❖ 2 c sugar
- ❖ 1 T honey
- ❖ 1 pt white wine 2 qt seven-up
- ❖ 1 dash of lemon
- ❖ 1 dash of cognac (or triple -sec)

Mix strawberries, sugar & honey and let set 1-2 hours. Add the wine, seven up and dash of lemon and leave set another hour or so. Just before serving add a dash of cognac.

REFRESHING PUNCH

➤ FRUIT TEA PUNCH

Yield 75 Servings

- ❖ 1 ga weak tea
- ❖ 2 c sugar
- ❖ 2 qt water
- ❖ 2 qt apple juice
- ❖ 2 cn (46-oz) pineapple juice
- ❖ 1 cn (20-oz) pineapple,Crushed
- ❖ 1 pt lemon juice
- ❖ 1 cn (12-oz) orange juice,Frozen
- ❖ 2 c strawberries,Frozen -optional
- ❖ 1 qt ginger ale

Mix all ingredients together except ginger ale. Add ginger ale just before serving. Serves 75.

REFRESHING PUNCH

➤ FRUITY ISLAND PUNCH

Yield 1 Servings

- ❖ 2 qt cranberry-apple juice
- ❖ 1 qt orange juice
- ❖ 1 qt pineapple juice
- ❖ 3 qt carbonated lemon-lime -beverage
- ❖ 1 qt vodka (or rum (optional))

Mix chilled juices together in large punch bowl or crock with spigot. Add liquor and ice. Add carbonated drinks just before serving.

REFRESHING PUNCH

➤ FRUITY SHERBET PUNCH

Yield 15 Servings

- ❖ 4 c apple juice, chilled
- ❖ 4 c pineapple juice, chilled
- ❖ 4 c orange juice, chilled
- ❖ 2 l ginger ale, chilled
- ❖ 2 qt orange (or pineapple -sherbet)

Combine juices in a punch bowl. Stir in ginger ale. Top with sherbet. Serve immediately.

REFRESHING PUNCH

➤ GALA FRUIT PUNCH

Yield 1 Servings

- ❖ 2 cn limeade concentrate,Frozen -thawed (6 oz. each)
- ❖ 1 cn orange juice,Frozen -concentrate,thawed (6 oz.)
- ❖ 1 cn lemonade concentrate,Frozen - (6 oz.),Thawed
- ❖ 1 cn pineapple juice,(46 oz.)
- ❖ 2 c cranberry juice cocktail 3 c cold water
- ❖ 1 qt frozen strawberries,thawed
- ❖ 2qt ginger ale,chilled
- ❖ 1qt club soda,chilled

In punch bowl, combine concentrates, juices and water; stir well. Stir in strawberries, ginger ale and club soda. Serve immediately. Yield twenty-five (1-cup) servings.

REFRESHING PUNCH

➤ GARDEN PUNCH

Yield 10 Servings

- ❖ 1 bn lemon balm sprigs,on long -stems, if possible
- ❖ 2bn milk-flavored mints,on long - stems, if possible
- ❖ 1cn unsweetened pineapple juice -or
- ❖ 46z unfiltered apple juice or -apple cider
- ❖ 2juice of lemon
- ❖ 1lemon,cut in thin slices
- ❖ 1sparkling water (or -champagne) - to taste

Gently wring the bunches of lemon balm and mint to release the flavor. Place in a large glass pitcher, cover with the juices and the lemon slices. Chill overnight, occasionally stirring and pressing down on the herbs with the back of a wooden spoon. Pour into iced glasses with a splash of sparkling water or champagne and a sprig of fresh lemon balm or mint.

Makes about 10 4-oz servings.

REFRESHING
PUNCH

➤ GARDEN TEA PUNCH

Yield 0 Servings

- 1 c water
- 2/3 c sugar
- 2 T fresh mint, snipped
- 1 c orange juice
- 1/2 c lemon juice
- 2 c strong brewed tea
- 1   1-liter bottle club soda -chilled
- 1 lg stem lavender (or borage) -(optional)
- rose,;; calendula,or;;
- pansy petals,(optional) flower ices cubes (or ring)
- -(optional)

Place water, sugar, mint, and lavender or borage, if desired, in a large stainless-steel or nonreactive pan. Bring to boiling; remove from heat and let steep for 20 minutes. Strain mixture through 100%-cotton

REFRESHING PUNCH

cheesecloth-lined colander.

Add orange juice, lemon juice, and tea to flavored water; chill. Just before serving, add chilled club soda. If desired, sprinkle punch with flower

REFRESHING PUNCH

petals and serve with flower ice cubes or ring. Makes about 3 quarts or 16 (6-ounce) servings.

Flower Ice Cubes Fill ice-cube trays half full with water and place an edible blossom or petal on water in each cube. Freeze until firm, then fill the tray with water and freeze again.

Flower Ice Ring Fill ring mold half full with water and place edible blossoms or petals on water in ring. Freeze until firm, then fill the mold with water and freeze again.

REFRESHING PUNCH

➤ GENEVA'S PARTY PUNCH

Yield 50 Servings

- ❖ 1 stephen ceideburg
- ❖ 46 oz pineapple juice,unsweetened
- ❖ 24 oz lemonade concentrate,Frozen
- ❖ 12 oz limeade concentrate or
- ❖ -orange juice,concentrate 36 oz water
- ❖ 2 l sugar-free lemon-lime soda

Mix pineapple juice, lemonade and limeade. Pour over ice just before serving; add water and lemon-lime soda.

REFRESHING PUNCH

➤GIBBSVILLE'S PUNCH

Yield 1 Servings

- ❖ 1 pk cherry kool aid
- ❖ 1 pk strawberry kool aid
- ❖ 2 c sugar
- ❖ 3 qt water
- ❖ 6 oz frozen orange juice,Canned -concentr,ate
- ❖ 6 oz frozen lemonade,Canned
- ❖ 1 qt ginger ale

REFRESHING PUNCH

➤ GINGER ALE PUNCH

Yield 1 Servings

- ❖ 2 lg cans unsweetened pineapple -juice
- ❖ 1 cn lemonade and 3 cans,Frozen -water
- ❖ 1/2 cn limeade and 2 cans,Frozen -water
- ❖ 1 cn orange juice and 2,Frozen -cans wate,r
- ❖ 1 c sugar
- ❖ 4 qt dry ginger ale
- ❖ 2 qt soda water
- ❖ 1 pt strawberries (or use,Frozen -mint le,aves)

Mix base of juices and sugar. Chill. Just before serving add ginger ale and soda.

REFRESHING PUNCH

➤ GINGER ALE-SHERBET PUNCH

Yield 50 Servings

- ❖ 6 qt ginger ale
- ❖ 7 pt sherbet (mint (or orange)) 2 or
- ❖ 3 pt vanilla ice cream (optional)

Combine 1 quart ginger ale and 1 pint sherbet, beating well before adding any more. Continue adding in these proportions as needed. For extra "body" to the punch, add 2 or 3 pints of vanilla ice cream every so often.

Yield 50 (1/2-cup) servings.

REFRESHING PUNCH

➤ GINGER AND BLOOD ORANGE PUNCH

Yield 12 Servings

- 8 oz fresh ginger, peeled
- 1/2 c honey
- 1/4 c lemon juice
- 8 blood oranges - (to 10)
- 1 c bourbon
- 1 Blood Orange and Pomegranate -
- Ice Ri,(see recipe)
- 12 Candied Orange Swizzle -Stick,(see recipe)

Chop ginger into 1 inch pieces. Place in a heavy-bottomed saucepan with 8 cups of cold water. Slowly bring to a boil over medium high heat, reduce heat to medium low, and simmer for 20 minutes.

Remove gingered water from heat, add honey and lemon juice, and stir. Cool completely in refrigerator. Juice oranges to yield 2 cups, strain juice, and chill. Strain the chilled ginger mixture into the orange

REFRESHING
PUNCH

juice.

Add bourbon, if desired and chill in a punch bowl with a Blood Orange and Pomegranate Ice Ring. Garnish each cup with a Candied Orange Swizzle Stick, and serve.

Makes 12 servings.

REFRESHING PUNCH

➤ GINGER APPLE FRUIT PUNCH

Yield 1 Servings

- ❖ 50 g fresh ginger
- ❖ 1 1/2   bottles water
- ❖ 3 c sugar,(3 to 4)
- ❖ 2 c apple concentrate
- ❖ 2 c fresh orange juice
- ❖ 1 c pineapple juice
- ❖ 1/4 c strawberry pulp a pinch of salt

Grind 50 gms of cleaned, fresh ginger to a rough paste or small pieces.

Boil 2 bottles of water , after the water starts bubbling add the ground ginger.

Add the sugar.

Boil on high flame for two minutes and switch off. Strain the ginger juice through a fine muslin.

Cool and then pour into another larger vessel, being carful not to pour

REFRESHING PUNCH

to the end. Thus the sediment and impurities remain to be thrown away.

Strain once more and add in the rest of the juices and strawberry pulp.

This concentrate must be refrigerated and can be blended with iced water or soda to make an incredible summer drink at short notice.

REFRESHING PUNCH

➤ GINGER TROPICAL PUNCH

Yield 16 Servings

- 1 1/2 c water
- 1 c sugar
- 2 T ginger root, chopped
- 4 whole cloves
- 1 whole cinnamon stick
- 6 oz orange juice, Frozen -concentrate
- 1/2 c orange juice, freshly -squeezed
- 1 whole orange, thinly sliced
- 1 whole lemon, thinly sliced

In a medium saucepan combine water, sugar, gingerroot, cloves, and cinnamon. Bring to boiling over medium heat, stirring constantly.

Reduce heat and simmer, incovered, for 5 minutes. Cool mixture; cover and let steep in refrigerator for several hours. Meanwhile, prepare apple and orange juices according to product instructions. In a large container combine the apple juice, orange juice, and lemon

REFRESHING PUNCH

juice. Cover and chill.

Strain steeped ginger mixtrue. In a punch bowl stir together the fruit juices and ginger mixture. Reserve 8 lemon or orange slices. Foat remaining fruit slices in the punch. Cut reserved fruit slices in half. Garnish each cup with half a fruit slice and an orange curl (optional), if desired.

REFRESHING
PUNCH

➤ GLORIA'S PUNCH

Yield 1 Servings

- ❖ 1 lg cans orange juice,Frozen -prepared as directed
- ❖ 2 lg cans pink lemonade,Frozen -prepared as directed
- ❖ 2 lg cans unsweetened,Frozen -grape juice,prepared as di
- ❖ 2 lg cans five alive fruit,Frozen - punch,prepared as directe
- ❖ 2 l gingerale
- ❖ 2 oranges,Sliced

Mix juices and gingerale together. Float orange slices on top.

REFRESHING PUNCH

➤ GLORIOUS CHRISTMAS PUNCH

Yield 1 Servings

- ❖ 1 3 oz. pkg. cherry gelatin
- ❖ 1 c water, Boiling
- ❖ 1 6 oz. can lemonade, Frozen
- ❖ 3 c cold water
- ❖ 1 qt cranberry juice cocktail -chilled
- ❖ 1 12 oz. bottle ginger ale -chilled

Dissolve gelatin in boiling water; stir in lemonade. Add cold water and cranberry juice. Place two trays of ice cubes in a large punch bowl; pour punch over ice. Pour in ginger-ale.

REFRESHING PUNCH

➤ GLUGG "HOLIDAY" PUNCH

Yield 1 Servings

- 1 bottle
- 1 bottle
- 1 stick cinnamon
- 12 allspice berries --,Cracked
- 12 whole cloves
- 12 caramoms -- optional
- 1 rind and juice of 1 orange
- 1 to 2 cups
- 1 currants,figs, -- and 1 dates)
- 1 c whole almonds
- 1 c akvavit (or vodka)
- 1 dry red wine
- 1 white wine
- 1 fruit (raisins,Dried

REFRESHING
PUNCH

Combine wines in large enamel pot. Tie spices in cheeese-cloth. Add Orange rind, orange juice, fruit and nuts. Bring to a boil. Reduce heat immediately to simmer. Simmer for 1 hour. Pull out spice bag and orange rind. Add Vodka or Akvavit. Serve warm, with portion of fruit in each cup. Store leftover in jar in refrigerator for up to 3 months.

REFRESHING PUNCH

➤ GOLDEN AZTEC PUNCH

Yield 6 Servings

- ❖ 3/4 c sugar
- ❖ 1/2 c lime juice
- ❖ 1/2 c orange juice
- ❖ 1/2 c water
- ❖ 1 c ice, Crushed
- ❖ 1 1/2 c chilled club soda

In blender container, combine all ingredients except club soda; blend until slushy.

Pour mixture into pitcher. Stir in club soda. Yield 6 (3/4 cup) servings.

REFRESHING PUNCH

➤ GOLDEN GATE PUNCH

Yield 14 Servings

- ❖ 250 ml lemon juice
- ❖ 250 ml orange juice
- ❖ 250 ml grape juice
- ❖ 60 ml liquid sucaryl
- ❖ 1 l water

Combine all ingredients and chill well. Serve over ice cubes, crushed ice, or a ring mold of ice. Garnish with lemon or orange slices, as desired. Makes 14 servings (approx. 125ml each).

REFRESHING PUNCH

➤ GOLDEN GLOW PUNCH

Yield 25 Servings

- ❖ 1(6 oz.) can lemonade,Frozen - concen,trate, thawed
- ❖ 1(6 oz.) can orange,Frozen -juice co,ncentrate, thawed
- ❖ 1 (6 oz.) can,Frozen -tangerine juice,,concentra
- ❖ 2 c cold water
- ❖ 2 (33 oz.) bottles ginger ale- chille,d
- ❖ 1 ice cubes (or ice mold)

In large nonmetal pitcher or punch bowl, combine juice concentrates and water; mix well.

Just before serving, add ginger ale and ice; stir to blend. Garnish as desired. Yield 25 (1/2 cup) servings.

REFRESHING PUNCH

➤GOLDEN PUNCH

Yield 30 Servings

- ❖ 1 c freshly squeezed lemon juice
- ❖ 6 c orange juice
- ❖ 8 c apple juice
- ❖ 4 c sugar syrup, or sweeten to -taste
- ❖ 1 qt orange sherbet (optional)

Combine all ingredients and chill. Add 1 quart orange sherbet just before serving, if desired. Yield about 30 servings.

To make sugar syrup, mix equal parts of water and sugar in a saucepan over low heat; stir until sugar is dissolved.

REFRESHING PUNCH

➤ GOLDEN SUMMER FRUIT PUNCH

Yield 1 Servings

- ❖ 1 cn (12-oz) orange juice,Frozen -concent,rate
- ❖ 1 cn (12-oz) lemonade,Frozen -concentrate
- ❖ 1 cn (48-oz) apricot nectar
- ❖ 1 cn (48-oz) pineapple juice
- ❖ 1 bottle (2-liter) ginger ale

Dilute the orange juice and lemonade as directed on can. Mix with remaining ingredients. Yield about 2 gallons.

REFRESHING PUNCH

➤ GOLDEN SUMMER PUNCH

Yield 100 Servings

- ❖ 3 cn (12 oz.) orange juice,Frozen - concen,trate
- ❖ 3 cn (12 oz.) lemonade,Frozen n-concentrat,e
- ❖ 6 3/4 qt water
- ❖ 6 cn (12 oz.) apricot nectar
- ❖ 6 cn (28 oz.) pineapple juice
- ❖ -(3-48 oz cans)

Mix.

REFRESHING PUNCH

➤ GOLLEEE GELATIN PUNCH

Yield 12 Servings

- ❖ 1 6 oz box strawberry jello
- ❖ 2 c water, Boiling
- ❖ 2 c cold water
- ❖ 1 c sugar
- ❖ 1 pt cranberry juice
- ❖ 1 2-liter bottle ginger ale

Dissolve the gelatin in the boiling water. Add the sugar and stir until the sugar dissolves, but do not boil. Add the cold water and let the mixture cool, but not congeal. Pour into a punch bowl and add the cranberry juice. Add the ginger ale just before serving.

REFRESHING PUNCH

➤ GRADUATION PUNCH

Yield 1 Servings

- ❖ 1 cn fruit drink,Frozen -concentrate,thawed
- ❖ (12 oun 1 cn orange juice,Frozen
- ❖ -concentrate,thawed (6 ounc
- ❖ 1 cn lemonade concentrate,Frozen
- ❖ - (6 ounces),Thawed
- ❖ 2 l ginger ale
- ❖ 1 qt orange sherbet

In a punch bowl or large container, combine the fruit punch, orange juice, and lemonade concentrates. Stir until well mixed. If not serving right away, cover and refrigerate. Just before serving, add the ginger ale and sherbet.

REFRESHING PUNCH

➤ GRANNY'S HONEY PARTY PUNCH

Yield 12 Servings

- ❖ 1/4 c honey
- ❖ 1/4 c water, Boiling
- ❖ 3 c water
- ❖ 3 c unsweetened pineapple juice
- ❖ 3/4 c orange juice
- ❖ 1/4 c lemon juice
- ❖ 1/4 c fresh mint, Lightly Packed -leaves
- ❖ 1 l ginger ale, chilled Ice ring

In a large bowl, combine honey and 1/4 cup boiling water until combined. Stir in 3 cups water, fruit juices, and mint. Cover; chill at least 4 hours.

Discard leaves before serving. Pour punch into a punch bowl; stir in ginger ale. Carefully slide ice ring into punch bowl. Garnish each serving with fruit on a decorative pick, if desired.

REFRESHING PUNCH

➤ GRANNY'S PUNCH

Yield 4 Servings

- ❖ 1 qt cranberry juice
- ❖ 1 qt lemonade
- ❖ 1 qt pineapple juice
- ❖ 1 qt (or less) lemon lime soda or
- ❖ 1 qt (or less) ginger ale

Pour all of the juices together in a big punch bowl. Add enough soda to give the punch a kick, but not so much that the flavor of the juices is diluted.

REFRESHING PUNCH

➤ GRAPEFRUIT-STRAWBERRY PUNCH

Yield 15 Servings

- ❖ 8 oz grapefruit, Frozen -concentrate
- ❖ 2 lb strawberries, frozen, thawed
- ❖ 2 qt ginger ale
- ❖ 1 ice cubes

Crush strawberries. Place in bowl. Reconstitute grapefruit juice. Pour over strawberries; add ice and ginger ale.

REFRESHING PUNCH

➤ GREEN PUNCH

Yield 12 Servings

- ❖ 1 pk lime kool aid
- ❖ 1 lg can limeade
- ❖ 1 1/2 c sugar
- ❖ 2 c water
- ❖ 1 pk lime kool aid, prepared
- ❖ 4 c water
- ❖ 1 qt ginger ale
- ❖ 1 pt lime sherbet

Mix 1 pk lime kool aid, 1 can frozen lime aid, sugar and water. This can be made ahead. Prepare second package of kool-aid. Freeze in ring mold.

When ready to serve mix lime mixture, 4 cups water, ginger ale. Mix in punch bowl. Add frozen kool aid ring and sherbet.

REFRESHING PUNCH

➤ GUAVA PUNCH

Yield 12 Servings

- ❖ 1/2 c sugar
- ❖ 1/2 c water
- ❖ 1 1/2 c guava juice
- ❖ 1/4 c orange juice
- ❖ 1 1/2 T lemon juice
- ❖ 1/2 c pineapple juice
- ❖ 1 t orange rind, Grated
- ❖ 1 bottle (28-oz) ginger ale -chilled

Combine sugar and water in a saucepan and simmer 10 minutes; cool. Stir in juices and rind; chill. Before serving, add ice and ginger ale. Makes 12 (4 oz.) servings.

REFRESHING PUNCH

➤ HALLOWEEN PUNCH

Yield 1 Servings

- ❖ 4 c apple cider
- ❖ 1 1/2 c orange juice
- ❖ 1 c pineapple juice
- ❖ 2 T sugar
- ❖ 4 c ginger ale
- ❖ 1 ice cubes

1) Stir together the apple cider, orange juice, pineapple juice and sugar in a punch bowl.

2) Pour in the ginger ale. Add ice cubes.

Makes 10-1/2 cups.

REFRESHING PUNCH

➤ HARBOUR ISLAND RUM PUNCH

Yield 1 Servings

- ❖ 1 1/2 oz dark rum
- ❖ 1 oz orange juice
- ❖ 1 oz pineapple juice 1 oz grapefruit juice
- ❖ ¼ lime, freshly squeezed
- ❖ 1 ice

Combine all ingredients. Pour over ice. May easily be made in quantity by doubling, tripling, etc. all ingredients. Yield 1 drink.

REFRESHING PUNCH

➤ HARVEST PUNCH

Yield 1 Servings

- ❖ 1 cn orange juice,Frozen.-concentrate,(6,oz.) thawe
- ❖ 1 cn lemonade concentrate,Frozen - (6 oz.),Thawed
- ❖ 1 cn pineapple juice,Frozen -concentrate,,(6 oz.) thawe
- ❖ 10 c ,water
- ❖ 6 whole,cloves
- ❖ 2 cinnamon sticks

Combine all ingredients in a 4-quart saucepan. Simmer over low 10 to 15 minutes. Lift out cloves and cinnamon and discard. Serve hot. If desired, punch can be served in a scooped-out pumpkin

REFRESHING PUNCH

➤ HAWAIIAN LUAU PUNCH

Yield 1 Servings

- ❖ 1 cn (46 oz) pineapple juice
- ❖ 1 cn guava nectar
- ❖ 1 cn papaya nectar
- ❖ 1 qt ginger ale
- ❖ 1 qt mint (or lime sherbet)

1) Freeze opened cans of juice just past the mushy stage.

2) Pour it and the ginger ale over sherbet in a punch bowl.

Makes 1 gallon.

REFRESHING PUNCH

➤ HAWAIIAN PUNCH

Yield 25 Servings

- ❖ 3 cn large hawaiian punch,Frozen
- ❖ 3 cn large lemonade,Frozen
- ❖ 2 cn large orange juice,Frozen
- ❖ 1 qt rasberry sherbert
- ❖ 2 qt ginger ale

In a LARGE punch bowl, follow can directions for each frozen juice. Spoon in rasberry sherbert and whip it up. Pour the ginger ale slowly around the edge of the punch bowl (2 bottles).

REFRESHING PUNCH

➤ HEALTH-KICK PUNCH

Yield 1 Servings

- ❖ 1 juice of 10 oranges
- ❖ 1 juice of 6 lemons
- ❖ 6 md or 4 large bananas,sliced
- ❖ 1/2 c pineapple,Crushed
- ❖ 1 1/2 c light rum
- ❖ 1 c honey
- ❖ 1 c banana-flavored liqueur
- ❖ 2/3 c grenadine syrup
- ❖ 6 dr angostura bitters
- ❖ 1 lemon,Slices

Combine first 9 ingredients in a large bowl, stirring well. Pour punch mixture, one-third at a time, into container of electric blender; blend until smooth. Pour punch into large serving container; stir well. Float lemon slices on top of punch; serve over crushed ice. Yield about 3 quarts.

REFRESHING
PUNCH

➤ HIBISCUS TEA PUNCH

- ❖ 8 hibiscus (or Red Zinger tea) -bags
- ❖ 4c water, Boiling
- ❖ 1 1/2 c sugar (or honey)
- ❖ 1 bottle sparkling cider -
- ❖ -(25.4 oz), chilled
- ❖ Lemongrass (or lemon wedges) -to garnish

Place the tea bags in a large container. Add the boiling water and let steep 10 minutes. Remove the tea bags; add the sugar or honey while the tea is hot. Refrigerate until ready to use.

Add the sparkling cider. Serve in tall glasses over ice. Garnish with lemongrass or lemon wedge.

REFRESHING PUNCH

➤ HILTON PUNCH

Yield 1 Servings

- ❖ 1 oz club soda
- ❖ 2 oz orange juice
- ❖ 2 oz pineapple juice
- ❖ 2 oz sweet and sour mix
- ❖ 2 oz cranberry juice.

Option 1 pour one scoop ice with ingredients into blender. Option 2 pour ingredients on the rocks.

Garnish with one slice of orange, wheel of lime, maraschino cherry. Great for a party punch bowl, too.

REFRESHING PUNCH

➤ HOLIDAY DELIGHT PUNCH

Yield 1 Servings

- ❖ 1 cranberry cocktail juice
- ❖ 1 pineapple juice
- ❖ 1 hawaiian fruit punch
- ❖ 1 qt ginger ale

Mix all ingredients and chill.

REFRESHING PUNCH

➤ HOLIDAY DRINKS - BRANDY MILK PUNCH

Yield 1 Servings

- ❖ 1 1/2 oz brandy
- ❖ 1t brown sugar dissolved in one - teaspo,on of
- ❖ 1,water
- ❖ 4oz plain milk,up to 5
- ❖ 1pinches nutmeg

Shake all ingredients with ice and strain into a high ball glass over ice.

Dust with Nutmeg.

REFRESHING PUNCH

➤ HOLIDAY FRUIT PUNCH

Yield 3 Servings

- 1 lb red, green or blue/black
- 1. grapes
- ½ pineapple, peeled & cubed
- 3 c white wine
- 3 c cranberry juice cocktail
- 3 T lemon juice
- 3 T sugar
- 1 qt club soda, lemon-lime soda
- 1. (or champagne)

Fill ring mold (any size that fits into punch bowl) with 1 to 1 1/2 pounds of grape clusters of all colors. Barely cover with water; freeze. Halve and seed the remaining grapes. Put into a large refrigerator container, along with pineapple. Add remaining ingredients except soda or champagne. Cover and chill two hours or overnight. At serving time, dip ring mold in hot water for ten seconds; remove ice

REFRESHING PUNCH

ring. Put into punch bowl. Pour in fruit-wine mixture. Add soda water or champagne. Ladle punch and some fruit into cups.

Makes about 3 quarts.

REFRESHING PUNCH

➤ HOLIDAY PUNCH

Yield 8 Servings

- ❖ 1 3/4 c chilled lemon-lime soda -(about 30 o,unces)
- ❖ 3 c chilled cranberry-apple -juice drink
- ❖ 1 c chilled dry white wine
- ❖ 2 T brandy

Combine all ingredients in large bowl. Stir until well blended. Add ice just prior to serving. Try floating some fresh strawberries in the punch for a nice presentation. For a non-alcohol punch substitute Apple Cider for the White Wine and skip the Brandy in entirety.

REFRESHING PUNCH

➤ HOMECOMING PARTY PUNCH (SERVES 100)

Yield 100 Servings

- ❖ 6 c sugar
- ❖ 4 boxes lemon jello,(3 oz.)
- ❖ 6 oz orange juice,Frozen
- ❖ 6 oz frozen lemon juice,or
- ❖ 6 oz realemon
- ❖ 2 cn pineapple juice,(46 oz.)
- ❖ 1 1/2 oz almond extract
- ❖ 4 qt ginger ale
- ❖ 1 ga water

Combine sugar and 4 cups water. Cook until dissolved. Add Jello and dissolve. Add frozen fruit juices and pineapple juice. Add 1 gallon water and almond extract. Let stand. Use 2 quart mixture to 1 quart ginger ale.

Makes 12 quarts punch.

REFRESHING PUNCH

➤ HOT "TAILGATE" PUNCH

Yield 1 Servings

- 1 ga apple cider
- 1 sm condensed orange -juice(frozen)
- 1/3 c brown sugar
- 5 whole cloves,to 6 -cloves
- 2 cinnamon sticks,to 4 -sticks

Combine ingredients and simmer 1 to 2 hours. Serve in crock pot or in a cleaned out pumpkin. Pumpkin keeps punch warm but does not change the flavor of the punch.

REFRESHING
PUNCH

➤ HOT BUTTERED PUNCH

Yield 1 Servings

- 3/4 c brown sugar
- 4 c water
- 1/4 t salt
- 1/4 t nutmeg
- 1/2 t cinnamon
- 1/2 t allspice
- 3/4 t cloves, Ground
- 2 lb cans jellied cranberry sauce
- 1 qt pineapple juice Cinnamon sticks Butter

In slow-cooking pot, combine brown sugar with water, salt, nutmeg, cinnamon, allspice, and cloves. Break up cranberry sauce with fork. Add cranberry sauce and pineapple juice to pot. Cover and heat on low for 3 to 4 hours. Serve hot in individual mugs with cinnamon sticks. Dot eachmug with butter.

REFRESHING PUNCH

➤ HOT CHRISTMAS PUNCH

Yield 1 Servings

- ❖ 64 oz bottled apple juice
- ❖ 64 oz bottle cranberry juice
- ❖ 5 cinnamon sticks, broken
- ❖ 5 oranges, sliced 1/4 thick

Place all ingredients into a large stainless kettle and bring to a boil. Reduce heat and simmer 45 minutes to 1 hour. Strain and serve hot. Do store in plastic containers.

REFRESHING PUNCH

➤OT CIDER PUNCH

Yield 12 Servings

- ❖ 2 qt apple cider
- ❖ 1/2 t cinnamon
- ❖ 1/2 t mint
- ❖ leaves 1/4 t nutmeg
- ❖ 1/2 c powdered sugar
- ❖ 2 whole oranges, sliced
- ❖ 1 cloves
- ❖ 1/2 c apricot brandy (or other) -spirits

1) In a large saucepan combine cider, cinnamon, mint, nutmeg and sugar.

2) Stud orange slices with cloves; add to cider.

3) Simmer very slowly, do not boil.

4) The longer it simmers, the better.

5) Just before serving, add brandy or other spirits.

Makes 12 to 16 servings.

REFRESHING PUNCH

➤ HOT CRANBERRY PUNCH

Yield 10 Servings

- ❖ 4 c unsweetened pineapple juice
- ❖ 4 c cranberry juice
- ❖ 1/2 c brown sugar, Packed
- ❖ 1 c water
- ❖ 1 t whole cloves
- ❖ 1 cinnamon stick

Tie cloves and cinnamon stick in cheesecloth. Combine all ingredients in crock-Pot. Cover and cook on Low setting for 4 to 10 hours. Serve hot, in punch cups.

REFRESHING
PUNCH

➤ HOT FRUIT PUNCH

Yield 1 Servings

- ❖ 1 pt cranberry juice cocktail
- ❖ 1 cn (no. 2) pinapple juice
- ❖ 1/2 c water
- ❖ 1/3 c dark brown sugar
- ❖ 1/2 T whole cloves
- ❖ 3 2-inch sticks of cinnamon -(break in,small pieces)

Place all ingredients in a six-cup percolator (glass). Do not use metal pot. Let come to a boil. Reduce heat, simmer 3 minutes, remove all spices except cinnamon stick pieces. Keep hot and serve.

REFRESHING PUNCH

➤ HOT HOLIDAY PUNCH

Yield 20 Servings

- ❖ 3 c apple juice
- ❖ 3 c orange juice
- ❖ 6 c cranberry juice cocktail
- ❖ 3/4 c maple syrup
- ❖ 2 t powdered sugar
- ❖ 1 1/2 t cinnamon
- ❖ 3/4 t cloves
- ❖ 3/4 t nutmeg
- ❖ 1 cinnamon sticks

Cinnamon sticks are optional but make a very pretty addition as stirrers in steaming hot mugs of punch. Combine all the ingredients in a very large heavy pan, except the cinnamon sticks. Bring to a boil and turn to simmer for few minutes. You can put the ingredients in a crockpot after it has boiled and keep warm over low heat.

HOT MILK PUNCH

Yield 1 Servings

- 1 parts baileys
- ½ part cognac
- 1 1/2 t (7 ml) sugar
- 3 parts hot milk
- 1 ds nutmeg, Freshly Ground

Combine Baileys and cognac to dissolve sugar. Add hot milk and stir. Sprinkle with nutmeg.

REFRESHING PUNCH

➤ HOT MULLED FRUIT PUNCH

Yield 14 Servings

- ❖ 6 3-in cinnamon sticks
- ❖ 5 whole cloves
- ❖ 1/2 t whole allspice
- ❖ 3 teabags
- ❖ 2 bottle,(32 oz) white grape -juice
- ❖ 1 bottle,(32 oz) apple juice
- ❖ 5 sm macintosh apples

Abt 30 minutes before serving. Wrap spices in pieces od double thickness cheesecloth to make spice bag, tie with string. In 5 qt saucepan over high heat, heat teabags , spice bag, white grape juice, apple juice and 2 cups water to boiling. Reduce heat to low, cover and simmer 20 minutes. Discard tea bags and spice bag. Place apples in 4 qt heat safe punch bowl. Pour hot mixture over apples.

Makes about 14 cups.

REFRESHING PUNCH

➤ HOT OR COLD PERKY PUNCH

Yield 1 Servings

- 46 oz pineapple juice
- 1 qt cranberry juice
- 3 c water
- 6 cinnamon sticks
- 2 T whole cloves
- 1 T whole allspice
- 1/2 t salt
- 1 c brown sugar

Pour fruit juice and water into 30-36 cup automatic coffee maker. Place remaining ingredients in basket.

Plug in coffee maker and perk. Makes 25 - 4 ounce servings. May be served hot or cold.

REFRESHING PUNCH

➤ HOT PINEAPPLE PUNCH

Yield 9 Servings

- 1 cn 46-oz unsweetened pineapple
- 1/2 c sugar
- 1/4 c lime juice
- 1/4 t nutmeg, Ground
- 3 1/4 c dry white wine
- 1 cinnamon sticks
- 1 fresh pineapple

In large saucepan, combine pineapple juice, sugar, lime juice, and nutmeg; bring to boiling, stirring till sugar dissolves. Reduce heat; stir in wine. Heat through but DO NOT BOIL. Pour into heat-proof glasses or mugs. Garnish each serving with cinnamon stick stirer and pineapple wedge. Makes about 9 cups.

REFRESHING PUNCH

➤ HOT PUNCH

Yield 1 Servings

- 1 cn (6oz) orange juice,Frozen -concentrate
- 1 cn (6oz) lemonade,Frozen
- 1 1/2 c sugar
- 10 c water
- 1 t almond flavoring
- 1 t vanilla

Combine all ingredients, heat and serve.

REFRESHING PUNCH

➤ HOT SCARLET WINE PUNCH

Yield 1 Servings

- 1 bottle cranberry juice-cocktail,
- 32 oz 4 cups
- 1/3 c brown sugar,packed
- 1 2 inche sti cinnamon
- 4whole cloves
- 1bottle white zinfandel -750-milliliter

In a large saucepan, combine cranberry juice cocktail, brown sugar, cinnamon stick and cloves.

Bring to boiling; reduce heat and simmer, uncovered, for 5 minutes. Remove spices. Add white zinfandel. Heat till just warm.

Ladle into mugs or transfer to a warm, heatproof pitcher and pour into mugs.

Makes 14 servings.

REFRESHING PUNCH

➤ HOT SPICED CRANBERRY PUNCH

Yield 1 Servings

- ❖ 1 Lemons,thickly sliced
- ❖ 24 Whole cloves
- ❖ 6 c Cranberry juice cocktail
- ❖ 2 c Lemonade,fresh or made from concentrate,Frozen
- ❖ 1/2 t cloves,Ground
- ❖ 1/2 t cinnamon,Ground
- ❖ 1/2 t allspice,Ground
- ❖ 1 c Sugar (or honey)
- ❖ 12 Cinnamon sticks,(optional)

Stud the lemon slices with the whole cloves to float on the top of the punch. In a large enameled or nonreactive pot, combine the cranberry juice, lemonade, cloves, ground cinnamon, allspice, honey, and cinnamon sticks, if you are using them, and simmer the punch over low heat for 15 minutes.

REFRESHING
PUNCH

Serve in a 2- to 3-quart punch bowl, or keep the punch warm in a deep chafing dish or an electric cooking pot. Offer the cinnamon sticks as swirlers, if desired. this recipe yields 2 quarts of punch.

REFRESHING PUNCH

➤ HOT SPICED FRUIT PUNCH

Yield 8 Servings

- ❖ 4 c cranberry-raspberry drink 2 c orange-strawberry-banana -juice
- ❖ 1 t whole allspice
- ❖ orange-and-spice tea bags
- ❖ 5 lemon rind strips,(3 x -3/4-inch)
- ❖ 1 cinnamon stick,(3-inch)
- ❖ 1/4 c sweetened cranberries,Dried - (such as craisins)
- ❖ 1/4 c dried apricots,Diced 2 T sugar cinnamon sticks,(optional)

1. Combine first 6 ingredients in a large saucepan; cook mixture 30 minutes over medium-low heat. Remove from heat; let stand 30 minutes. Strain mixture; discard solids. Return juice mixture to pan; stir in cranberries, apricots, and sugar. Cook over medium-low heat 30 minutes, stirring occasionally. Pour into mugs; serve with a cinnamon stick, if desired. Yield 8 servings (serving size 3/4 cup).

REFRESHING
PUNCH

➤ HOT SPICED PERCOLATOR PUNCH

Yield 10 Servings

- ❖ 3 c water
- ❖ 3 c pineapple juice
- ❖ 1 T whole cloves
- ❖ 1/2 T allspice, whole
- ❖ 3 sticks cinnamon, broken
- ❖ 1/4 t salt
- ❖ 1/2 c brown sugar

Put water and pineapple juice in bottom of an 8 cups percolator and the rest of the ingredients in the top. Perk for 10 minutes until spices permeate. Serve hot in mugs or punch cups.

REFRESHING PUNCH

➤ HOT SPICED PUNCH

Yield 1 Servings

- ❖ 1 heesecloth
- ❖ 3 sl fresh ginger
- ❖ 8 whole cloves
- ❖ 4 cardamom seeds,(optional)
- ❖ 1 stick cinnamon
- ❖ 1 ga apple cider
- ❖ 1 pt pineapple juice
- ❖ 1 pt orange juice
- ❖ 6 lemons,sliced
- ❖ 3oranges,sliced

Cut cheesecloth into a 6-inch square to form a spice bag. Place ginger, cloves, cardamom and cinnamon into square. Tie corners together. Place spice bag and remaining ingredients into large Dutch oven. Bring to a boil. Reduce heat and simmer 15 minutes stirring occasionally. Serve warm. Yield 5 quarts.

REFRESHING PUNCH

➤ HOT SPICY LEMONADE PUNCH

Yield 10 Servings

- 3 c cranberry juice
- 2/3 c sugar
- 12 oz can lemonade concentrate -thawed
- 4 c water
- 2 T honey
- 6 whole cloves
- 2 cinnamon sticks, broken
- 1 lemon, sliced and unpeeled

In slow-cooking pot, combine cranberry juice, sugar, lemonade concentrate, water and honey. Tie cloves and cinnamon in small cheesecloth square. Add spice bag and lemon slices to juices.

Cover and cook on low for 3 to 4 hours. Remove spice bag. Keep hot in slow-cooking pot.

REFRESHING PUNCH

➤ HOT WEATHER PUNCH

Yield 1 Servings

- ❖ 6 oz orange juice,Frozen -concentrate,th,awed
- ❖ 6 oz lemonade concentrate,Frozen -,Thawed
- ❖ 5 cn (6 oz. ea.) water
- ❖ 12 oz apricot nectar
- ❖ 2 1/2 c pineapple juice

Pour orange juice and lemonade concentrates into a 2 1/2 - 3 quart pitcher. Add water, nectar and pineapple juice, stirring. Chill. Makes about 2 ½ quarts.

REFRESHING PUNCH

➤ HOT WHISKEY PUNCH

Yield 1 Servings

- ❖ 1 3/4 c irish whiskey
- ❖ 1/4 c (packed) golden brown sugar
- ❖ 6 thick lemon,Slices
- ❖ 24 whole cloves
- ❖ 3 c hot water

Mix whiskey and sugar in pitcher to dissolve sugar. Divide among 6 heatproof glasses. Stud each lemon slice with 4 cloves. Place 1 slice ineach glass. Pour 1/2 cup hot water into each; stir to blend.

REFRESHING PUNCH

➤ HOT WINE CRANBERRY PUNCH

Yield 11 Servings

- ❖ 1 pt cranberry juice cocktail
- ❖ 1 c water
- ❖ 3/4 c sugar
- ❖ 1 cinnamon sticks
- ❖ 6 whole cloves
- ❖ 1 bottle Burgundy wine - -4/5-qt.
- ❖ 1 lemon,thin slices unpeeled

Combine ingredients in slow-cooking pot. Heat on low for 1 to 2 hours. Strain and serve hot. May be kept hot and served from slow-cooking pot set on lowest setting.

REFRESHING PUNCH

➤ ORANGE-PEACH PARTY PUNCH

Yield 30 servings

- ❖ 1/2 c sugar
- ❖ 1/2 c water
- ❖ 2 sticks cinnamon
- ❖ 1/4 c lime juice
- ❖ 1 orange-peach juice, 64oz
- ❖ 1 chilled
- ❖ 1 bottle sparkling water
- ❖ 1 hilled
- ❖ 1 bottle champagne, sparkling
- ❖ 1 white wine or 1 liter of
- ❖ 1 gingerale
- ❖ 1 chilled
- ❖ 1 frozen orange wedges

REFRESHING PUNCH

Prepare Frozen Orange Wedges Cut two thin slices from small orange. Cut each slice into 8 wedges; place in a single layer on plate. Cover with plastic wrap and freeze until serving time.

Heat sugar, water and cinnamon to boiling; reduce heat. Cover and simmer 15 minutes. Cover and refrigerate at least 2 hours or until chilled.

Remove cinnamon from syrup. Just before serving, mix syrup with remaining ingredients in punch bowl. Garnish with Frozen Orange Wedges.

REFRESHING PUNCH

➤ IRISH COFFEE-EGGNOG PUNCH

Yield 3 Servings

- 2 qt refrigerated eggnog
- 1/3 c brown sugar,firm packed
- 3 T coffee granules,Instant
- 1/2 t cinnamon
- 1/2 t nutmeg
- 1 c irish whiskey
- 1 qt coffee ice cream
- 1 sweetened whipped cream
- 1 nutmeg,Freshly Grated

Combine eggnog, brown sugar, instant coffee and spices in a large mixing bowl; beat at low speed with an electric mixer until sugar dissolves. Chill 15 minutes; stir until coffee granules dissolve and stir in whiskey.

Cover and chill at least 1 hour. Pour into punch bowl or individual

REFRESHING PUNCH

cups, leaving enough room for ice cream. Spoon in ice cream. Garnish each serving as desired with whipped cream and nutmeg.

REFRESHING PUNCH

➤ ISLAND FRUIT PUNCH

Yield 4 Servings

- ❖ 2 1/4 c orange juice
- ❖ 1 c pineapple juice
- ❖ 1/2 c light rum
- ❖ 1/4 c fresh lime juice
- ❖ 2 T grenadine syrup

Combine first 4 ingredients in a pitcher; stir well, and chill. Fill 4 glasses with orange juice mixture. Slowly pour 1-1/2 teaspoons grenadine syrup down inside of each glass (do not stir before serving).

Yield 4 cups (serving size 1 cup).

REFRESHING PUNCH

➤ ISLAND RUM PUNCH

Yield 1 Servings

- ❖ 1 oz White (or golden rum)
- ❖ 1 T Lime juice, or to taste
- ❖ 2 t Sugar, preferable raw, or -more, To Taste
- ❖ 1 oz Water
- ❖ Ice cubes

In a short cocktail glass, mix together rum, lime juice, sugar, and water. Add ice cubes and stir. Adjust amount of lime and sugar to taste. This recipe yields 1 serving.

REFRESHING PUNCH

➤ JACK CONNOR'S ARTILLERY PUNCH

Yield 1 Servings

- ❖ 2 qt vodka
- ❖ 2 qt brandy
- ❖ 2 qt dry red wine
- ❖ 2/3 qt orange juice
- ❖ 1/3 qt lemon juice
- ❖ 1 1/4 c sugar
- ❖ 8 qt sparkling water

Combine all & add 8 quarts sparkling water.

REFRESHING PUNCH

➤ JAMAICAN RUM PUNCH

Yield 18 Servings

- 1 c lime (or lemon juice (sour))
- 2 c grenadine syrup (sweet)
- 2 c jamaican white rum (strong)
- 1 c light rum (strong)
- 2 c pineapple juice (weak)
- 2 c orange juice (weak)
- 1/2 t nutmeg, Grated

Remember the formula 1 portion of sour, 2 portions of sweet, 3 portions of strong, 4 portions of weak.

Mix together ingredients at least 1 hour before serving. This punch looks beautiful served in a punch bowl with a pretty ice ring layered with orange slices & cherry halves. Makes 18-20 servings.

REFRESHING PUNCH

➤ JANE GLASS' PUNCH

Yield 20 Servings

- ❖ 1 cn (large) pineapple juice
- ❖ 1 cn (small) pineapple juice
- ❖ 1 cn (large) orange juice
- ❖ 1 cn (small) orange juice
- ❖ 1 cn (small) grapefruit juice
- ❖ 1 1/2 oz citric acid (or lemon juice)
- ❖ 1 c sugar
- ❖ 2 qt water
- ❖ 1 qt ginger ale

Mix all ingredients except ginger ale. Chill. Just before serving, add ginger ale.

REFRESHING PUNCH

➤ JELLO PUNCH

Yield 100 Servings

- 9 c sugar
- 9 c water
- 6 pk jell-o
- 6 c water, Boiling
- 6 c cold water
- 3 cn pineapple juice, large
- 3 bottles lemon juice, 8 oz
- 1 1/2 oz almond extract
- 3 bottles ginger ale, 32 oz

Boil sugar and water, Dissolve jello in 6 cups boiling water and add 6 cups of cold water. Add sugar to jell-o Add pineapple juice, lemon juice and almond extract When ready to serve add ginger ale

REFRESHING
PUNCH

➤ JUBILEE PUNCH YIELD 12

Servings

- ❖ 1 1/2 qt orange juice
- ❖ 1 1/2 c lemon juice
- ❖ 1/3 c maraschino cherries, with -juice
- ❖ 2 1/2 sparkling white grape juice- 750 ml each

Mix orange and lemon juices with cherries. To serve, place in large punch bowl with large block of ice and add grape juice.

www.ingramcontent.com/pod-product-compliance
Lightning Source LLC
LaVergne TN
LVHW010203070526
838199LV00062B/4486